PITY MY SIMPLICITY

PITY MY SIMPLICITY

*The Evangelical Revival and the Religious
Education of Children 1738–1800*

PAUL SANGSTER

LONDON
THE EPWORTH PRESS

FIRST PUBLISHED IN 1963

© THE EPWORTH PRESS 1963

Book Steward
FRANK H. CUMBERS

PRINTED AND BOUND IN ENGLAND BY
HAZELL WATSON AND VINEY LTD
AYLESBURY, BUCKS

for

PAULA

Gentle Jesus, meek and mild,
Look upon a little child,
Pity my simplicity,
Suffer me to come to Thee.

CHARLES WESLEY

ABBREVIATIONS

Poetical Works = *The Poetical Works of John and Charles Wesley*, edited by G. Osborn (1868)

Works = *The Works of John Wesley*, published by the Wesleyan Conference Office (1872)

Preface

I AM under a debt of gratitude to three people.

My Father, the late Rev. Dr W. E. Sangster, M.A., LL.D., encouraged me to pursue a line of research and approved this one. Though he died before the work had advanced beyond a chaotic mass of notes, he would have liked the result because of his one lack of judgement: like Charles Wesley, and with as little cause, he showed a marked partiality for his own children.

Dr J. D. Walsh, M.A., of Jesus College, Oxford, has been extremely kind, nor could the work ever have been attempted without his guidance. He has shown himself unsparing of his time, utterly selfless in providing references, and patient beyond belief. If no other end had been in view I would still have found the study worth while to have been fired with his own enthusiasm.

Miss Dorothy Dunningham, of Westminster College, Oxford, typed the work for me. She both offered to do it and did it in her own spare time. I am extremely grateful to her.

The Staff at the Bodleian Library, where most of the research has been done, have been as helpful as their reputation led me to expect. In the British Museum Reading Room and the Epworth House Library, City Road, London, I received equal courtesy.

In its original form—very different from the present one—this book was a thesis approved by the Theological Faculty of the University of Oxford for the degree of Bachelor of Letters.

P. E. SANGSTER

WESTMINSTER COLLEGE
OXFORD

Contents

CHAPTER I

The Evangelicals

THE EVANGELICAL fathers are still with us. Their whiskery faces peer sternly down in chapel vestries; families treasure the Bibles they owned and tell proudly how Wesley, or Whitefield, or Grimshaw preached in this very Chapel; children still sing their hymns in Sunday-schools, or attend their great foundations.

Few of them were teachers, and none left a permanent mark on the history of education. Wesley alone has been seriously considered as an educator, and usually considered only to be dismissed contemptuously.

Yet somehow they passed their tradition on, and somehow they must have been successful, for the power of Evangelicalism today is a tribute to their educational abilities.

This book attempts to tread the path those children trod. It is often a gloomy one, strewn with the skulls of the happy ones who died young and died well. Indeed, it would be easy to sneer at the religious education which prepared this path through life. Much seems repressive: hell is ever held before infant eyes; attendance on death-beds seems almost a means of grace. Yet if the Evangelicals do not appear at their best in training children, they had excellent reasons for much they did. If death-beds are omnipresent in these pages, so were deaths. If hell is a constant threat, might not the threat prevent the reality? The chief characteristic of the Evangelicals is their earnestness. And to us the faults of their system are often the very fruit of it.

Further, my theme is limited to the years that were commonly the tormented ones. Childhood fears often led to mature years of happiness—a short time of anguish for decades of bliss. But the bliss is unrepresented. Adult happiness is no concern of mine here.

And it is not all anguish. Life was not only misery for them, and here and there the warmth of personality transcends theory, and makes an antetaste of heaven on earth. It is with the personalities of the Evangelicals that I introduce the subject, seeing first the Fathers in their historical context, so that, later on, the children may be understood.

'The history of the Evangelical Revival', said Canon Smyth, 'is essentially a history of personalities'.[1] If John Wesley, the greatest man of his age, if not of the post-apostolic age, was an evangelical, so was 'mad Will Darney', the illiterate itinerant who converted Grimshaw; if George Whitefield, the greatest preacher of modern times, was one, so was George Bell, who proclaimed the end of the world and died an atheist; if Augustus Toplady, who wrote 'Rock of Ages, cleft for me' and yet became a scurrilous 'religious' pamphleteer, was one, so was his opponent —John Fletcher—Vicar of Madeley, undisputed saint of Protestantism. There were nobles, like the Countess of Huntingdon; cobblers, like Thomas Olivers; men as wealthy as the Thorntons; as wise as Henry Venn and as foolish as Thomas Maxfield; an ex-slave-trader in John Newton, a reclaimed sailor in Silas Told, an ex-pot boy in George Whitefield, an ex-mason in John Nelson; men who were formerly High Churchmen, Roman Catholics, or completely outside any form of religion; men who, still Evangelicals, finished their ministries in the Church of England, in Methodism, in every form of Dissent. Paradoxically, the only personal quality they appear to have in common is uniqueness.

Had all these men found their ideas from one source, their unity in first principles would be, in the light of their variety, surprising but at least explicable. Since, however, they came from separate springs, the source of the main Church of England stream being neither Wesley nor

Whitefield, the task of explaining the origins of this extraordinary movement is still undone.

The Evangelical Revival was, at least in part, a violent
reaction against the religion of the times, so the state of the
Establishment before 1738 demands brief mention.

It would be easy to paint too black a picture of the
Church which the Evangelicals revived. Montesquieu's
famous remark that 'in England there is no religion, and
the subject, if mentioned in Society, excites nothing but
laughter' might well be true of the limited Society he
met, but it was not universally true. In all ages a few men
at least kept alive the spark of vital religion, and this was
true of the eighteenth century.

The prevailing mood was undoubtedly latitudinarian, and
deism was popular among the fashionable class. The archaic
machinery of the Church of England which permitted
political bishops, gross unfairness in salaries, pluralism
and non-residence, was helpless to deal with the problem,
and the ejections of 1662 and 1689 creamed off the best
of the clergy, till 'only the cautious and the colourless
remained'.[2]

All this can be admitted. But it is also true that this
period saw the growth of the SPCK, the SPG, and all the
work of the Charity Schools and the Anti-Vice campaigns.
The stress was on Works and on Morality, and it was finally
on this ground that the Evangelicals at the end of the
century met the reviving body of the main Church.

The Age of Reason found any form of heart religion
unacceptable. Such an extraordinary (albeit scriptural!)
title as *The Nature, Folly, Sin and Danger of being Righteous
over-much*' (a pamphlet by Dr Trapp) was readily understood and appreciated by the eighteenth-century readers.
But what the eighteenth century did believe in, and did
support very strongly, was benevolence, charity in all its
forms. This, and little more than this, was eighteenth-
century piety. Parson Woodforde was the ideal shepherd, and ideal sheep pledged their support for Charity

Schools. Children were the most obvious targets for benevolence.

Against this background, not wholly dark, the Revival began. What had the early Evangelicals in common?

First, there was the conviction that nothing except religion mattered. This is most easily seen in Wesley and Whitefield and the earliest Evangelicals. The conviction sprang, not from reason, which might well have persuaded them otherwise, but from their emotions. W. H. Proby called the first motto of their party 'heart-religion rather than form-religion'. The truths of Christianity 'required not only to be defended, but to be applied to the heart and life',[3] and this was the work the Evangelicals set themselves. Henceforward experience, not reason, was to be the chief test of religion, and experience told the Evangelicals that religion was not '*an* essential of life' but '*the* essential of life'.[4]

The Evangelicals lived their faith. They believed it, talked of it, indeed, talked of little else and shunned every snare that might prevent them living it absolutely. Hence, at least in part, the opposition to them. They were different. They kept themselves to themselves.

Secondly, and an inevitable corollary of the first, Evangelicals were militant propagandists. Having found their own salvation, they longed to share it with others. More, they forced others to share it by every means in their power. 'I felt my soul', writes Henry Longden, 'trembling in birth for the salvation of perishing men',[5] or, for that matter, perishing children. And the means of grace were headed by 'The Pulpit'. When the people would not come to the churches to hear them or they were not allowed to preach, with Wesley they 'consented to become more vile', and preached in barns, or at market-places, or in fields, wherever they could get a hearing.

Thirdly, deep in the souls of the Evangelicals was fear of the world. They became world forsaking. Yet their division between the Natural and the Regenerate man was

not the horrible dichotomy of Swift's Yahoos and Houy-
hnhnms, a mad inhuman division, but a determination to
cling on to the spiritual part of man, and make all else subservient to it. That it was attainable, however difficult, the
life of John Fletcher proved. Life in the world, yet beyond
the dross of it, was the goal of them all.

Fourthly, the Evangelicals believed in the isolation of,
and great emphasis on, the Doctrine of Personal Salvation.

Theologically the Evangelicals had little to say. 'Had
Evangelicalism been distinguished by a more systematic
theology and Evangelicals by less individuality ...' laments
one historian.[6] Surely it is the very reaction against the
religion of the day that makes them such poor theologians.
The niceties of theology the latitudinarian Church discussed happily and fully. And what did it profit them?
When Church scholarship is wedded to religious indifference, what is the good of it? The Evangelicals were too
absorbed in the one essential thing to care very much about
speculative argument. 'They conceived of religion primarily
as a subjective relationship between the individual soul and
God';[7] nothing more was needful. If only they had never
forsaken this tacit belief, they would have been spared the
disastrous Calvinistic Controversy, which proved how
tenuous was their hold on theology.

The centre of their belief was 'a faith in Jesus crucified
and that only'; hence the enormous stress on the doctrine of
Salvation, and a tendency to preach on that to the exclusion
even of the Resurrection and the Ascension. Almost all
their preaching was directed to this one end, though Wesley
in his own way and others in different ways made provision
for the souls that were saved. The world of difference
between the attitudes of the Evangelical and the Latitudinarian is seen in their methods of preaching. 'Ah,' says a
constant church-goer in Whitefield's biography, 'I heard
one of those preachers at our church. He preached such
a sermon! It was almost an hour long, and he said down-
right that all unconverted people were in a state of damna-

tion, and would go to Hell, if they did not believe on the
Lord Jesus! Truly, he set the parish in an uproar, for we
are not used to such sort of preaching. Thank God for a good
parson, say I; for the Sunday after, our parson (God bless
him!) preached a sermon against such doctrine; and,
though he was no longer than a quarter of an hour, he
made us all easy again. He told us we were in no danger of
going to Hell, and that there was no fear of our being
damned, for we were all good Christians, if we paid every
one their own, and did as we would be done by.'

Fifthly, the Evangelicals were alike in their weak hold on
Church order and practice. The Church, they believed, was
the sum of God's elect, not a collection of nominal Christians
with a particular label. The earlier Evangelicals exchanged
pulpits happily with Dissenters—which many of them became, and some always were—and many of them preached
in the streets and fields. There was sufficient consecration,
they considered, in the presence of God at their meetings,
and His omnipresence made a barn or a field as holy as a
church. Though some of the earlier Evangelicals had found
considerable difficulty in preaching outside the Establishment, it was not until the time of John Venn and Simeon
that the difficulty became almost insuperable.

Lastly, the Evangelicals believed in Social Christianity.
When some of their earlier stresses were not quite so dominant—when some thought that life did contain a little more
than religion; when the earlier exclusiveness had lost some
of its isolation, then the evangelical stress on works of
charity became all the more obvious. They joined whole-
heartedly in the Sunday-school Movement, made their contribution to the Charity Schools, joined the war against vice,
founded their own schools, and were in the vanguard of
most social movements of the latter half of the eighteenth
century. They had led in visiting prisons and attending the
condemned, in making good literature available to all, and
later, they led the campaign against slavery.

The unity of the Evangelicals received a terrible blow in

1770 when Whitefield, who moved freely among all forms of Evangelicals, died, and so began the Calvinistic Controversy, perhaps the most bitter, the most futile, and the most damaging theological dispute of the century. Its bitterness, regretted by all the participants later, except Fletcher, who wrote nothing to regret, made a mockery of their religion; the problem of God's foreknowledge and man's freewill is an insoluble one which greater minds had abandoned in despair; and it turned the Evangelical cause, a union which cut across all other divisions, into a battleground of abuse.

There were never many High Calvinists among the Evangelicals except at the height of the Controversy, when polemical bad temper forced men to say more than they intended. Whitefield would not be a good example, since he often contradicted himself, and even appears to have preached universal salvation when he claimed to be a Calvinist. Romaine, perhaps, was the most consistent.

Most of the Church of England Evangelicals—but not the Wesleys or Fletcher, who were Arminians—were Moderate Calvinists. Since they had few theologians in their ranks, their views are difficult to analyse and appear to vary somewhat according to the writer. Their friends would say they accepted the core of Calvinism, but rejected its harsher side; their enemies that they refused the logical conclusions of their own system.

The followers of Whitefield, organized by that Mother in Israel, Lady Huntingdon, followed the Calvinistic theology and contained many Dissenters in their numbers. Though Lady Huntingdon attempted to use a chapel for her preachers under the wing of the Establishment, she failed, and when she was forced to license it under the Conventicle Act as a Dissenting Chapel and formed the Countess of Huntingdon's Connexion in 1782, separation from the Church of England was almost complete.

The secession of Methodism was more complicated. Though it was debated in the Methodist Conferences of 1755, 1756, 1761, 1778, and 1786, Wesley was always opposed to it, and died urging his followers to remain in the fold.

Nevertheless, as Wesley well knew, it was inevitable, and he himself had made it so. Nor can one see how he could have acted except as he did. His own singleness of purpose had made him careless of the authority of the Church from 1738. He was forced in 1787 to register his chapels as Dissenting places of worship, and in 1788 permitted worship in Methodist chapels to be held during church hours. Separation could not long be delayed, yet he tenaciously withstood it. The surest move in the inevitable schism, however, had been Wesley's ordination of his own preachers in 1784. 'Ordination is separation,' said Lord Mansfield, and Charles Wesley (always a stauncher Churchman than his brother) added his comment in verse:

> *How easily are Bishops made*
> *By man or woman's whim*
> *Wesley his hands on Coke hath laid,*
> *But who laid hands on him?*

Methodists had now to decide to which body their allegiance chiefly lay.

In 1791 Wesley died, leaving the problem unsolved, and the chaos did not resolve itself into Separation for some years. It was not, therefore, until the very end of the century that the Evangelical cause was irretrievably split.

Old habits die hard, and habits of thought hardest of all, and we therefore find little trace in religious education, even at the turn of the century, of variation in Church allegiance. Their common ground was always greater than their differences.

Finally, the numerical strength of the Evangelicals needs brief mention. In 1738 they could be counted on the fingers of one hand. By Wesley's death in 1791 there were well over 500 Church of England Evangelical Clergy, more than 200 Itinerant Methodist Preachers, and a host of Dissenting Evangelicals. By 1800 the Evangelicals were an important

Church Party. Methodism was strong and influential, and most forms of Dissent were vigorous. In 1737 Evangelicals did not exist, yet little more than half a century later they were a dominant influence in England. What they taught their children, therefore, is of tremendous importance: the faith they handed on is relevant to our understanding of all succeeding generations.

REFERENCES

1. C. Smyth, *Simeon and Church Order*, p. 6.
2. G. R. Balleine, *A History of the Evangelical Party in the Church of England*, p. 13.
3. Abbey & Overton, *The English Church in the Eighteenth Century*, II, p. 58.
4. M. G. Jones, *Hannah More*, p. 89.
5. *Life of Henry Longden, of Sheffield, by himself*, p. 41–2.
6. M. G. Jones, *Hannah More*, p. 97.
7. Ibid. p. 230–1.

CHAPTER II

The Evangelicals and Children

RELIGIOUS EDUCATION IN THE EIGHTEENTH CENTURY

SOME HISTORIANS have suggested that religious education before the Evangelical Revival was virtually nonexistent. They have been answered by others who proved, easily enough, that even in those dark days a few good men taught religion well. Nobody doubts, however, that in general, education was dispensed 'by the indigent and uninstructed' and 'moral education consisted ... of mechanically acquired knowledge of the Bible and the Catechism'.[1]

We need little imagination to picture the gentleman who, when asked what religious education he gave, replied, 'I hear them their catechism once a week', and, when pressed about how he gave moral instruction, answered: 'I tell them to be good lads, you know, and mind what I say to them, and so on.'[2] Men of that calibre are common enough: we could find plenty today. But we could not find a boy of ten waiting in prison to be executed with fifty-one others, as Charles Wesley did, and begin religious instruction there. If the Evangelicals seemed to blunder in regard to children, we do well to remember what sort of children they were. The vast majority were illiterate; many were filthy and foulmouthed; some were more beasts than children. And the religious instruction had to be for them, for they needed it most. Most theorists prescribed for the genteel few; the Evangelicals also prescribed for the needy many.

NON-EVANGELICAL THEORISTS

A brief mention must be made of the educational theory of the day. Though the eighteenth century made a considerable contribution to educational thought, religious education received scant treatment. Very little of this theory attracted the Evangelicals, whose distinctive views were largely outside the important trends of the history of education. Nevertheless, the current theories are important, even if the Evangelicals were more likely to react than to emulate.

Rousseau (1712–78) was the greatest educational theorist of the age, though his theories took a long time to percolate into England. When they did so, they were anathema, not only to Evangelicals, but to most Christians, for obvious reasons. Religious education, he believed, should be left very late, and here the Evangelicals parted company with him. 'A clergyman of Colchester followed Rousseau's system; his two sons died of intemperance before eighteen years of age.'[3] The story may or may not be true, but it illustrates the typical evangelical reaction to Rousseau.

Mrs Macaulay Graham (1733–91) found the Bible unsuitable as a foundation for juvenile reading, and so was found unsuitable by the Evangelicals. Vicesimus Knox (1752–1821), who offered a dull-sounding religious programme for schools (the catechism, Bible-study, reading of sermons and the regular recital of prayer), might have found favour in evangelical eyes had he not warned readers against 'enthusiasm'. He almost certainly aimed this shaft at Wesley. Joseph Priestly (1732–1804) had some influence with them through Hannah More, but closest to the Evangelicals in spirit was the Rev. G. Monro who, in *A Plea . . . for Christian Education*, published as early as 1711 and re-published in 1823, urges 'The Happiness of Early Piety', and Locke's important treatise on education was also respected. Locke, however, was primarily a philosopher, and his standpoint was widely opposed to theirs.

Curiously enough, the two strongest influences on Wesley, and through him on Evangelicalism in general, were foreign. The Schools of Port Royal, founded in 1646 (the technical founder, St Cyran, had died in 1643) and dissolved in 1660, were influential far beyond their short life. Their aim was 'to preserve their pupils in the innocence of their baptism'.[4] This was also Wesley's aim. So also was there a parallel in the gloomy view taken of original sin, yet an apparently repressive system was made gentle by the saint-liness of St Cyran, by the kindness of Wesley. Another parallel is the close supervision of children day and night, but the most striking is the subordination of all else in both systems to the worship of God. It was always rare to be 'serious'.

The other foreign influence was the Moravian School of Herrnhut in Germany. Again religious education was the central purpose of the school, and again, in order to prevent the spread of evil influence, absolute surveillance was the rule.

EVANGELICAL STRESS ON RELIGIOUS EDUCATION

All early evangelical education has religion as its primary object. 'You have nothing to do but save souls', said Wesley to his helpers and he particularized little further when, with special reference to education, he said that children are 'entrusted to your care, that you may train them up in all holiness, and fit them for the enjoyment of God in eternity'.[5]

Whitefield also stated this educational aim in a letter to Franklin: 'As we are all creatures of a day, as our whole life is but one small point between two eternities, it is reasonable to suppose that the grand end of every Christian institution for forming tender minds should be to convince them of their natural depravity, of the means of recovering out of it, and of the necessity of preparing for the enjoyment of the Supreme Being in a future state'. He explained the purpose of the Christian school as leading to conversion. Nor was conversion the deliberate aim only of the earliest Evangelicals. A retired schoolmaster from Poole went to Newfoundland in 1775. 'The people are willing that I should come and teach their children to read and write; and perhaps by this means they will in time be inclined to receive the Gospel'.[6] As late as 1802 a correspondent of the *Christian*

Observer, the father of several children who had died pious deaths, writes happily of occasions 'when the Spirit of God makes use of education as the means of producing sound conversion ...'.

This primary belief, that a religious life is the sole aim of man, explains all else in the theories of the Evangelicals. If all men must be saved, then literacy is essential. What hope has a man of standing fast in the faith if he cannot read his Bible? The means to the first aim of religious education, therefore, was the ability to read. A religious life was thought difficult for an illiterate.

Methodism's stress on a personal religion founded on the Bible demanded huge educational advances. Wesley's longing 'to instruct the ignorant, reform the wicked, and confirm the righteous' could only be answered by general literacy. Popular education owes much to the Evangelicals, most to Wesley himself.

Furthermore, if religious instruction has to be effective, then it must begin early, the earlier the better.

> *'Tis easier work if we begin*
> *To fear the Lord betimes,*[7]

wrote Watts. The Evangelicals seized the thought, and Rowland Hill virtually seized the words:

> *Happy the children who betimes*
> *Have learnt to know the Lord.*[8]

As a corollary to this, the Evangelicals repeatedly pointed out the dangers of neglect of religious instruction. That it was widely neglected cannot be doubted, but when the Evangelicals talked of neglect they often meant neglect of their own form of religious instruction, a very different matter. Wesley constantly drew his hearers' attention to the painful subject, and the saintly Fletcher, whose whole life was religion, makes the same complaint. The lamentation is heard continually.

There was another danger. Education might positively corrupt. 'Christians are imbibing so much of the cast and temper of the age, that they seem to be anxiously tutoring their children, and preparing them by all manner of means, not for a better world, but for the present'.[9] This was a terrible condemnation. It replaced God, the centre of all religion, by the World, almost synonymous with the Devil to the evangelical mind.

The way ahead, then, was clear. If education was God-centred all must be well. Yet the Evangelicals had doubts, Wesley perhaps more than any. There is more than an attributing of good things to God in his comments on the *Instructions for Children*, for which book he held great hopes. 'But nothing less than the finger of God can write it on their hearts', he concluded. There is a wistfulness here. Man is so fallible.

WESLEY'S THEORY OF EDUCATION

Wesley's theory came from three sources: he was a theologian, a theorist, and a pragmatist. All these approaches are important.

Theologically, his work in education had to fit into his general teaching, and Wesley's logical powers made them do so. His theory of man started with the original sin, into which we are all born. This depravity was never total in Wesley's theology because of his theory of Prevenient Grace. Grace in sufficient measure was given at Baptism, and the purpose of training was to keep the state pure after Baptism. The theory of Prevenient Grace avoided Calvinistic Determinism, which in Wesley's view would have made all training futile.

In theory, therefore, children who retained the purity of their baptismal state would need no second birth, and in a few cases of infant deaths Wesley supposes this is so, but his educational theory assumes that virtually all lose this state of grace during their early years. Education, therefore, battles with human depravity, and seeks to cure it.

It must also battle with it early, for grace is usually lost very soon after Baptism.

This is the simplest expression of Wesley's theological position. He frankly, and wisely, admits his inability to reconcile God's foreknowledge with man's free will: he is not clear on the amount of depravity which is in man, and he never states the relationship between Baptism and Prevenient Grace. Essentially, however, his system is clear and logical. He could justify it.

Beyond infancy children come into his adult theological system which demands Repentance, Justification by Faith, and Regeneration, as the successive steps in godliness. Beyond these lie Assurance and, offered to all but achieved by few, Entire Sanctification.

As a theorist Wesley sought far but found little to encourage him. Influence has been traced from Plato, Milton, and Locke, but none of the three was a practical educationist. His practical theories were influenced chiefly by the Port Royal Schools and the German school of Herrnhut, already mentioned. The latter's 'preposterous education', as Southey called it, was Wesley's chief influence in his theoretical approach, though a number of girls' schools in England appealed to him for their excellence, and Wesley's debt to Dr Doddridge's School was one he gratefully acknowledged.

It was as a pragmatist, however, that Wesley really worked. Most of his thought was the result of his own experience and experiments. His assumption that the state of baptismal innocence almost always departs was based on the fact that it happened to him. Similarly, he assumed that what was good educationally for him was the best for everybody. When we consider the system under which he was reared, we can only marvel at it. Susanna Wesley was, indeed, responsible for the pattern of his educational theory. He preached her advice, unacknowledged, in a sermon, and later he published her letter.

'In order to form the minds of children, the first thing to

be done is, to conquer their will', she writes. She repeats it. 'I insist upon conquering the wills of children betimes; because this is the only foundation for a religious education'. Again she repeats the point. 'I cannot yet dismiss this subject. As self-will is the root of all sin and misery, so whatever cherishes this in children, insures their after-wretchedness and irreligion: and whatever checks and mortifies it, promotes their future happiness and piety. This is still more evident, if we consider that religion is nothing else but the doing the will of God, and not our own. ... Heaven or hell depends on this alone. So that the parent who studies to subdue it in his children, works together with God in the saving of a soul: The parent who indulges it does the devil's work; makes religion impracticable, salvation unattainable; and does all that in him lies to damn his child, soul and body, for ever!'

Susanna Wesley still considers that her point is not made strongly enough. 'This, therefore, I cannot but earnestly repeat,—Break their wills betimes; begin this great work before they can run alone, before they can speak plain, or perhaps speak at all. Whatever pains it cost, conquer their stubbornness; break the will, if you would not damn the child. I conjure you not to neglect, not to delay this! Therefore (1) Let a child, from a year old, be taught to fear the rod and to cry softly. In order to this, (2) Let him have nothing he cries for; absolutely nothing, great or small; else you undo your own work. (3) At all events, from that age, make him do as he is bid, if you whip him ten times running to effect it. Let none persuade you it is cruelty to do this; it is cruelty not to do it. Break his will now, and his soul will live, and he will probably bless you to all eternity'.[10]

If this seems inhuman and cruel we have to remember that Wesley, who himself was brought up under it, is at great pains to commend it. It is the fruit of his great fallacy—that all boys were like him.

In fact Wesley was a most unusual boy. Reason—the very cause of the fallacy—was so imbued in him as a child that it became a family joke. He gave his will absolutely in submission to his parents. He had a Mother of remarkable ability and inflexible purpose. His own education led him to a Fellowship at Lincoln College and—what was more important—to know God's will and obey it. Such an education, he reasoned, must therefore be an ideal one, and what had succeeded for him must succeed for all.

There were certainly faults in the education he experienced at Charterhouse, where he believed he had lost his fellowship with God, but those faults could be rectified by a system which was really an extension of Susanna Wesley's family system—one which made God the centre of all work: which broke the will of the child in subjection to God; and which precluded all possibility of the devil interfering to claim the child for himself.

Such, then, was Wesley's educational theory. He experimented with it several times before the theory culminated in the establishment of Kingswood School. The success, or failure, of his theory can only be judged in reference to Kingswood, and that is considered in Chapter 4.

OTHER EVANGELICAL THEORIES

No other Evangelical was as systematic a theorist as Wesley. No other founded such a school as Kingswood and stamped his will upon it. Yet there were theorists among them, and there were practising teachers, and we can therefore find a pattern of training which is characteristically evangelical.

A number of Wesley's basic theories are echoed elsewhere. His theological view of the nature of children was common to them all, and held even more rigidly by the Calvinist majority. 'Teach them that they are sinful polluted creatures', parents were advised by the *Evangelical Magazine* in 1799 (p. 160) and Henry Venn's idea that 'the child is at first little more than an animal'[11] is a theological as well as a practical truth.

Most of the Evangelicals agreed with Susanna Wesley's insistence on breaking the wills of children. It was clearly a strongly held minority view of the eighteenth century, and Dr Johnson himself held it. Joseph Anderson, for instance, 'lamented over the inconsistency of such, as acknowledged the depravity of the human mind, and yet were unwilling ... to break the stubborn wills of their children'.[12] He claimed what had been claimed for more than half a century, that such parents 'have become the proverb of the day'. Samuel Walker of Truro shared the view but urged that 'our authority over our children' should not be 'for our own ends, but for God's glory in their spiritual welfare'.[13] Though affectionate towards children, Walker saw great danger in natural affection: he never married.

Henry Longden found it necessary to modify his views. 'At first ... believing that "just as the twig is bent the tree's inclined": he was disposed to censure warmly all religious parents without exception, whose children were refractory: but he was soon taught by sad experience to be more restricted in his expectations.'[14] What a pity John Wesley had no children!

The relationship of parents and children was systematized by the Evangelicals. Walker of Truro divided his precepts into 'Duty of Parents to Children', and 'Duty of Children to Parents'. Parents must be 'gentle towards them', while the children are 'cheerfully to submit to the corrections of their parents'. After this correction a child must 'be humbled for his fault', 'be grieved', 'submit to the reproof', and 'endeavour to recover God's favour and his parents' also'. The danger of the last injunction is an identification of the parents with God—more of that later.

Basil Woodd's system is more elaborate and more typically evangelical. The first of 'our obligations as parents' is 'To have Personal Religion', the second 'To show that they themselves are not of the world', the fifth 'To endeavour that children be not of this world', and injunctions are given to make this possible: 'Show the emptiness of the world', 'Make the home happy', 'Beware of the Society of the

World', 'Keep out of the habits of the world', and 'Occupy the time and the mind' with 'Benevolent engagements'.[15] The privileges of children, according to the same author, are 'federal interest in the Covenant', 'Initiation in good habits', and 'a general acquaintance with Christian doctrines and obligations'. One wonders if some of the children viewed these duties as privileges! One wonders also how much they suffered from the first 'obligations of children' which reads: 'They should know more than others'.

At least they were luckier than the youth who had to manage without such godly parents. Consider his plight on Judgement Day. 'But see! amidst the vast multitudes of lost souls, a frantic youth appears; despair is in his countenance, and fury in his soul! he has just discovered, amongst the number of the damned, his aged parents. Hark! he begins to curse them for leading him to that place of torment. "Behold (says he) my wretched mother" ...'.[16] We tactfully leave her guilt unexposed.

Death, of course, figures largely as a means of instruction. 'The great end of life is to be prepared for death',[17] and one could hardly begin soon enough. Isaac Milner was gentle with his child friends, yet he took his little niece to see a condemned felon at Carlisle. Even Fletcher's most characteristic way of teaching religion to his child correspondents was to remind them of the imminence of death.

'Present my respects to your son', he wrote to a Mother, 'and tell him, that last week I buried three young persons who had died of a malignant fever...'.[18]

Much depended, of course, on the manner of death. Gibbets had their uses, for you could tell the children that those 'whose crimes are made public, and whose persons are doomed to an ignominious death' were 'very early the despisers of God's word'.[19] Evangelicals preferred, however, a more seemly death, for 'if there be a moment when Christ and salvation, death, judgement, heaven and hell, appear more than ever to be momentous subjects of meditation, it is that which brings us to the side of a coffin containing the body of a departed believer'.[20] Children, therefore, had to view corpses, attend funerals, learn texts from gravestones by heart, and constantly remember: 'Time is short ... eternity is endless'.

Remarkably few Evangelicals faced the problem of making sure the children understood their teaching. One can only assume that many of them treated children precisely as they treated adults. William Hey, like some others, recommended 'Natural, easy, and frequent allusions to religious subjects',[21] but only Pratt seems to have realized what an extremely difficult thing they were attempting. His conclusions are interesting. 'Attention is to be kept up. The memory to be impressed. The judgement to be descended to. The affections are to be won. Volatility is to be fixed. How is this to be done? Anyhow. Even eccentricities may be useful here ... The question is, how to produce most effect?'[22]

Evangelicals probably produced most effect by the power of example. A few refer to its importance; the vast majority simply lived it. Whatever blunders they made in their teaching, there must have been great compensation in the saintly lives they led.

Some blunders, of course, were only the result of inexperience. A dying woman, assured she might be saved at the eleventh hour, rested content in the thought that 'she would be saved in eleven hours, and that was above two days ago'.[23] A more serious danger was that of giving children religious indigestion. Wise Henry Venn avoided it. 'The great danger is', he wrote, 'from surfeiting a child with religious doctrines, or over-much talk. Doctrines they are too young to understand; and too frequently talking to them is wearisome'. He considered it better to carry them 'to see an afflicted child of God, rejoicing in tribulation and speaking of his love'.[24]

Venn's *Complete Duty of Man*, written to supplement the famous *Whole Duty of Man*, rapidly became 'a manifesto of the Evangelical views'. For that reason alone it makes Venn's educational theory of great importance. His Chapter 27, 'The Duty of Parents towards their Children', is eminently sensible, and clearly written to assist all parents, for the evangelical note is not trumpeted loudly. He first asks for 'early habits of industry', with which all would agree; next for worldly provision to be made for children, which most worldlings would heartily endorse; and finally, having disarmed criticism, demands that parents 'above all others ... provide ... for the spiritual and everlasting welfare of their offspring'.

Again in Chapter 28, 'On the Method of Instructing Children', he begins circumspectly, suggesting what only nominal Christians would ask. He also distinguishes between poor parents and those of ampler means. At adolescence Venn plunges home his evangelical truths. 'By this time your children will have committed so many faults, have been so often corrected ... that you will have various striking proofs to convince them that they are creatures corrupted in their nature . . . and full of vile propensities.' They can see they need 'the Redeemer's interposition and merits'.

John Venn, his son, and a pillar of the Eclectic Society, largely followed his father's system, but gave more detail. His first precept of instruction was 'Engage the attention'. 'Images and stories are useful to engage attention,' he said. 'Teach but little. Fletcher of Madeley preached on robin redbreast and flowers.' John Venn did, however, make great demands on children's memories. 'I have known children get seventy chapters by heart. Perhaps the best way is thus to store the memory. Children are machines. Employ them properly.'[25]

James Stonhouse was another important theorist, his *Religious Instruction of Children Recommended* having a wide influence. Some of his advice strongly echoes Wesley. His simple exposition of religious teaching for children is a model of its kind. Children are to be told that 'God made all things, and knows all things; he sees us everywhere and is able to help us: he is gracious and merciful; we want his protection and care by night and by day, to keep us from evil, and to make us always safe and happy: we are sinful creatures and want forgiveness: we stand in need of his grace and help to do our duty: all Blessings are to be sought of God by prayer; he is to be praised for all the mercies that we receive; and all our hope of acceptance is on the account of Jesus Christ the Son of God, our Mediator'.

Rowland Hill was very successful with children, and his theory in part explains why. In *Instructions for Children* he urges that we 'first please, that afterwards we may profit'. His strong sense of humour, usually called levity or eccentricity by his contemporaries, enabled him to be more daring in his approach than many. We 'should be very righteous, but still not righteous over much', and children 'must be humoured in things that are innocent'. On the other hand, Rowland Hill could make most dangerous generalizations: 'And as children that are good always mind what is said to them, so it is they soon come forward in their learning: while wicked children, because they will not attend, are nothing better than dull or stupid blockheads.'

Henry Longden, a Sheffield Methodist, began with a rigorous system. Like Wesley, he wrestled to 'extirpate self-will and stubbornness in his children by the restraints of authority. None of them after the age of twelve months were suffered to indulge in childish pets'. It is recorded with pride that 'in his deportment ... there was no lightness nor jesting' and that 'he met his family statedly once a week, in the form of a class-meeting'. He lived long enough, however, to say of himself that he had been guilty of 'too frequent and severe correction' and it was said on his behalf that he 'lived to mature his plans and mode of education'.[26]

James Hervey's system differed in that he belonged, unlike the vast majority of Evangelicals, to the fashionable class. Music, therefore, was included in his children's curriculum; to most Evangelicals its study was too worldly to be safe. Nevertheless, evangelical thought is everywhere in his treatise. History is taught so that children can 'discern

how the fashion of this world passeth away', while geography
gives them 'magnificent thoughts of the great Creator'.[27]

Hannah More was both theorist and practical teacher.
Her theory began in the Doctrine of Depravity. 'If I were
asked what quality is most important in an instruction of
youth,' she wrote in *Strictures on the Modern System of Female
Education*, 'I should not hesitate to reply, such a strong
impression of the corruption of our nature, as should ensure
a disposition to counteract it.' All education she found
religious—and found secular subjects only useful in so far
as they qualified women for religious study. History 'is little
else than the story of the crimes of the human race'. One
curious part of her theory was that women were superior to
men since, not reading classical tongues, they were free from
pagan influence.

An early education she considered essential, holding with
Joseph Priestly the idea that early conditioning of certain
beliefs is essential for future happiness, and she also believed
that early instruction could 'make religion a lively pleasure
rather than a dry duty'.

With her theory she had a very strong common sense.
Laziness in children she thought the root of all evil, and she
had immense patience in instruction. 'How do you do the
thing?' said one to Miss More. 'I tell them the same thing
over and over and over again.'[28]

There remains among the Evangelicals one strange figure
who never had any theories and yet had remarkable success
in teaching children. Fletcher of Madeley was unique in
every way, and not least in his dealings with children. Many
commended his methods, but none could imitate him, for
only another Fletcher could do that successfully.

'His whole life was a sermon; all his conversations were
sermons,' said his biographer. Wesley called the same gift
a 'facility of raising useful observations from the most trifling
incidents'.[29] Neither gives the right impression. Fletcher
spoke to the iron-workers of Madeley about God hammering
their hard hearts; he wrote to little children about 'lumps of

heavenly sugar'; and on one occasion, eating his normal lunch in Switzerland, he ate and drank saying the words of the sacrament. Only a saint like Fletcher could have done it without blasphemy.

At another time he breakfasted at a girls' boarding-school, and found the fashionable meal lasted an hour. They came to share his breakfast soon after. He placed his watch on the table, ate his meal, showed them it had lasted a minute and a half and sang to them: 'Our life is a dream.' He concluded with 'a lecture on the value of time, and the worth of the soul'.[30]

'If I were not a minister,' Fletcher wrote to the local teacher, 'I would be a schoolmaster, to have the pleasure of bringing up children in the fear of the Lord.' He was, in fact, a schoolmaster, for he founded and taught in several Sunday-schools and he had special services for children.

His most extraordinary success was in places where one would least expect teaching to be done. 'I met some children in my wood,' he wrote during his tour abroad, 'gathering strawberries. I spoke to them about our common Father' (the children were Roman Catholics). They followed him home and people attempted to drive them away, 'saying I would not be troubled with children. They cried, and said they were sure I would not say so, for I was their good brother.' Fletcher saw them, of course, and they came to him daily. 'I make them little hymns, which they sing . . . Yesterday, I wept for joy on hearing one of them speak, as an experienced believer in Bristol would have done, of conviction of sin, and of the joy unspeakable in Christ that followed.'[31]

That this was no brief encounter of a day or two is proven by a letter of William Perronet, Fletcher's companion, written some time later. 'His [Fletcher's] chief delight seems to be in meeting his little society of children. He is exceedingly fond of them, and they appear to be as fond of him. He seldom walks abroad or rides out, but some of them follow him, singing the hymns they have learned, and conversing with him by the way.'[32]

The evangelical emphasis of all this is plain enough, but how Fletcher did it only Fletcher and God know. Of his young disciples he asked 'the faith of righteous Abel, the chastity of Joseph, the early piety of Samuel, the right choice of young Solomon, the self-denial and abstinence of Daniel'.[33] If it seems a heavy demand, we should remember that Fletcher, like Wesley, never made demands of others that he did not make of himself.

REFERENCES

1. E. B. Castle, *Moral Education in Christian Times*, p. 132.
2. J. L. & B. Hammond, *The Age of the Chartists*, p. 171.
3. J. H. Pratt, *Eclectic Notes*, p. 74.
4. H. C. Barnard, *The Port Royalists on Education*, p. 77.
5. *Works*, VII, 79.
6. *Wesleyan Methodist Missionary Society*, I, p. 266.
7. Watts' Hymns, 'The Advantage of Early Religion'.
8. Rowland Hill's Hymns 'The Blessings of a Godly Education'.
9. J. H. Pratt, *Eclectic Notes*, p. 272.
10. *Works*, VII, pp. 103–4.
11. Henry Venn, *Correspondence*, p. 249.
12. *A Short Account of Mr Joseph Anderson*, p. 29.
13. S. Walker, *Fifty-two Sermons*, II, III.
14. *Life of Henry Longden of Sheffield, by himself*, pp. 151–2.
15. J. H. Pratt, *Eclectic Notes*, pp. 389–90.
16. J. T. Barr, Sermon, 'Parental Duties Enforced'.
17. Josiah Hill, 'Sermon occasioned by the death of Richard Fisher'.
18. L. Tyerman, *Wesley's Designated Successor*, p. 138.
19. H. Venn, *Complete Duty of Man*, p. 238.
20. Legh Richmond, *The Dairyman's Daughter*.
21. John Pearson, *The Life of William Hey, Esq.*, Part II, p. 25.
22. J. H. Pratt, *Eclectic Notes*, p. 7.
23. *Evangelical Magazine*, 1800, p. 504.
24. H. Venn, *Correspondence*, pp. 422–3.
25. J. H. Pratt, *Eclectic Notes*, p. 7.
26. *Life of Henry Longden*, pp. 152–5.
27. James Hervey, *Works*, pp. 528–30.
28. J. H. Pratt, *Eclectic Notes*, p. 7.
29. L. Tyerman, *Wesley's Designated Successor*, p. 392.
30. Ibid. p. 98.
31. Ibid. p. 421.
32. Ibid. p. 425.
33. Ibid. p. 550.

CHAPTER III

The Method of their Teaching

THE EVANGELICALS used all the Methods they knew to inculcate religious principles in children. The most obvious, the most historically respectable, and the easiest was

CATECHIZING

This system, of course, had fallen into disuse during the first half of the eighteenth century, but was still observed by a few, nor were these few all like Thomas Jackson's master, who, as he catechized, 'stood before them with the book in one hand, and a substantial hazel-stick in the other'.[1]

It was natural that the Evangelicals should revive the almost obsolete custom, and virtually all of them used the method. They did more than this, however. They made it peculiarly their own and turned what could have been a barren and boring recital of essential truths into a lively method of instruction which children would not merely endure, but enjoy.

One vast improvement on 'vain repetitions' was to ask supplementary questions, both to make the information more interesting and to ensure that there was real understanding. John Crosse, for instance, varied the questions, and after them he had a Watts hymn and a prayer. His biography contains a whole chapter on his work as a Catechizer.[2] He used the system both on Sunday and one evening each week, and a typical passage is given. It begins:

'Mr C. Well, my dear children, how do you expect to be saved?

    A. By believing in the Lord Jesus Christ, Sir—
and it ends:
    Mr C. When must you repent and believe, children?
    A. Now, Sir, in childhood.
    Mr C. Why must you do it now, children?
    A. Because we may soon die, Sir.

This is clearly evangelical in tone, and if it sounds dismal to
us, it could not have seemed so to the children, for as soon
as the Sunday afternoon service finished, they 'like a swarm
of flies, would flock around him before the Communion
table', and afterwards, to 'escape' from their 'pious rudeness',
he hurried home to pray for them.

There is more than a hint in this account that Catechizing
had become virtually a children's service in itself. As time
went on this became a commonplace. Newton held children's
services, 'something of a catechetical nature', and their
popularity is attested by the presence, soon after its incep-
tion, of 'as many as 170, with some lookers-on'.[3] Mrs
Fletcher, widow of the Vicar of Madeley, preached every
Monday evening in preaching-houses of the neighbourhood,
and part of the service was catechetical exercises for the
children based on a pre-set passage of Scripture.[4]

A few of the Evangelicals, however, doubted the wisdom
of catechizing. Hanway did not want it in the Sunday-
school, or at least not for the younger pupils, while John
Venn began with a firm conviction that it was 'absurd to
teach children the catechism, which they did not compre-
hend' and bravely substituted his own system. He was
amazed, however, when he 'compared them with a stupid
maid-servant, who had been educated in the old way' and
found the servant much superior in knowledge. He then
returned to the 'old way'.[5]

The end of religious education for the Evangelicals was
not more religious knowledge. This was worthless. The only
true end for them was salvation, and—astonishingly—
salvation even through the Catechism is faithfully recorded.

An 'Anecdote' in the *Evangelical Magazine* of 1799 tells how a youth was 'convicted by being catechized' and Richard Hill tells how, as a child of eight or nine, while repeating the Catechism one Sunday evening, 'I found my heart sweetly drawn up to heavenly objects'.[6]

It is no wonder, then, that Catechizing should have been a chief means of Evangelical attack. It flourished amazingly. Hannah More 'advertised' it in her *Cheap Repository Tracts*, and the *Evangelical Magazine* often sounded its praises. It went so far as to claim that its neglect was the chief source of irreligion in England.

Like other means stressed by the Evangelicals, Catechizing soon became a fashion for the whole Church. None of the usual objections to Evangelical usages could apply to a system which had ancient traditions, and had merely fallen into disuse, and towards the end of the century the Bishop of Carlisle wrote a spirited tract on its observance, hoping it would 'remove the growing levity and lukewarmness in Subjects of this kind. . . .'

By 1880 all the Evangelicals had suitable Catechisms at their disposal, and a varied use of them might well prepare the children both for a full knowledge of their Christian beliefs and—much more important—for their personal Salvation.

If Catechizing cannot be claimed as more than a revival by the Evangelicals, their right to be considered as the originators with Watts of the English Hymn as it is known today is a strong one.

HYMNS

The great revival was born in song. An astonishing number of the Evangelical leaders were hymn-writers, and their hymns led to an important change in Public Worship. In place of the 'screaming of boys', 'the impertinence of a voluntary on the organ', and the 'scandalous doggerel of Hopkins and Sternhold', which Wesley so much detested, the Evangelicals were to enjoy hymns which contained 'all the important truths of our most holy Religion, whether speculative or practical . . . a body of experimental and practical divinity'.[7]

Not all the Evangelicals wrote hymns especially for children. Some, no doubt, would assume that children could understand and profit by the hymns of their elders, and others probably felt it beneath their dignity to write especially for children; those who did usually wrote an apologetic preface, as if to defend themselves from inevitable criticism. The chief reason, however, for the backwardness of Evangelicals here was their unwillingness to compete with Watts, whom all agreed had done it superlatively well.

Watts's *Divine Songs for Children* (1715), fiercely Puritan as they are, seemed to fill the needs of all serious Christians who wished their children to have a firm foundation in religion. As late as 1789 Mrs Trimmer published an edition of his *Divine and Moral Songs*, thus claiming their beliefs as her own. The songs were didactic, direct, and simple, and many of them were warnings (e.g. 'Against Scoffing and Calling Names', 'Against Swearing and Cursing', 'Against Idleness and Mischief', 'Against Evil Company', 'Against Pride in Clothes'). Even 'Love between Brothers and Sisters' (which contains the famous line 'Birds in their little nests agree') contains as much about the consequences of lack of love as it does about the love itself. Sulphurous flames abound.

> *Have ye not heard what dreadful plagues*
> *Are threatened by the Lord,*
> *To him that breaks his Father's Law*
> *Or mocks his mother's word?*
> *What heavy guilt upon him lies!*
> *How cursed is his name!*
> *The Ravens shall pick out his eyes,*
> *And eagles eat the same.*

Such hymns E. B. Castle sees as 'an attempt to replace physical punishment [for which the seventeenth century was notorious] with moral pressure'.[8]

Certainly 'moral pressure' was used by the Evangelicals;

hence their enormous respect for Watts's hymns. Thomas Adam used to present *Divine and Moral Songs* to children as gifts; John Scott, through reading the hymn 'The All-seeing God', affirmed, 'I was thus continually led to reflect on my guilt and danger';[9] while Robert Cecil records how 'when a child, and a very wicked one, too, one of Dr Watts's hymns set me crying in a corner'.[10]

Incomparably the greatest hymn-writer of his age—perhaps of all time—even Charles Wesley thought it necessary to preface his *Hymns for Children* by a full and interesting comparison between Watts's method and his own. 'There are two ways of writing or speaking to children: the one is, to let ourselves down to them: the other, to lift them up to us. Dr Watts has wrote in the former way, and has succeeded admirably well, speaking to children as children, and leaving them as he found them. The following hymns are written on the other plan: they contain strong and manly sense, yet expressed in such plain and easy language as even children may understand. But when they do understand them, they will be children no longer, only in years and in stature.' The false dichotomy with which the Preface opens and the extraordinary conclusion are in themselves a most telling commentary on the education of the age. Nor was Wesley really consistent in his theory. The exquisite

> *Gentle Jesus, meek and mild,*
> *Look upon a little child;*
> *Pity my simplicity,*
> *Suffer me to come to Thee*

is nearer what Charles Wesley claims as Watts's method rather than his own, while another verse of the same hymn, deleted in later editions—

> *Put Thy hands upon my head;*
> *Let me in Thine arms be stay'd;*
> *Let me lean upon Thy breast;*
> *Lull me, lull me, Lord, to rest*—[11]

is better than anything Watts wrote in Watts's own method.

Many of Wesley's hymns were written for special occasions (e.g. 'Before, or in, their work', 'Before reading the Scriptures', 'After School', etc.) and they are set out on a rough theological plan (beginning 'Of God', 'Of the Creation or Fall of Man', and so on). They give to the child a complete set of beliefs on the evangelical pattern, and since they were always considered important devotional literature as well as aids to Public Worship, their educational value was great.

Most children's death-bed accounts of the period contain quotations from Charles Wesley's hymns, sometimes justifying their certainty of heaven, sometimes in rapture at the prospect of their 'dissolution'.

The emphases are those we expect from the Evangelicals. The 'hell fire' residuum is present in many places, particularly in 'A Thought on Judgement' and 'On Hell':

> *There their tortured bodies lie,*
> *Scorch'd by the consuming fire;*
> *There their souls in torments cry,*
> *Rack'd with pride and fierce desire:*
> *Fear and grief their spirits tear,*
> *Rage, and envy, and despair.*[12]

Even in so doubtful an ability as freezing the blood of children, Charles Wesley knew no peer. This would be less strange if Charles Wesley habitually wrote about the horrors of hell; in fact he reserved his only full-blooded hell-fire hymn for the use of children ('The Cry of a Reprobate', an adult hymn, is milder). However, it would be unfair to exaggerate the horrors of Wesley's hymns for children. Considered as a whole, the hymns were remarkably fine, and the evangelical young were fortunate to be given a share in the 'noblest body of devotional verse in the English language'.[13]

Wesley had no able imitators. Few other Evangelicals attempted to write hymns for children, and those that did are best forgotten. Not until the turn of the nineteenth century did a later generation attempt it with success.

Rowland Hill's hymns for children, poor as they are, exercised a considerable influence for a few years and deserve brief mention. An imitation of Watts's hymns, they were originally written for Sunday-school children, but he explains in his Preface that he had them altered in style for 'Children of a superior description'—a very unhappy way of expressing it. They were revised and corrected by William Cowper, but judging by the finished products, one shudders to think what they were like in their unrevised state.

The collection is of forty six hymns and some oddments; the best are mediocre, the worst doggerel, and few of them show any ability at writing for children. Salvation—but never explained simply—is central:

> *But with Thy gracious power descend*
> *And all our sins subdue;*
> *O bid us to Thy sceptre bend,*
> *And form our souls anew.*

Children are not allowed to forget their condition of birth;

> *..... a sinner born,*
> *A child and heir of Hell,*

nor must they ever take credit for any cleverness, as the hymn 'After receiving Commendation' suggests, with its accompanying text, 'By the grace of God, I am what I am' (1 Cor. 15[10]).

Most of the remaining hymns for infant Evangelicals should never have been written, or at least not inflicted on children. They were perpetrated largely by various correspondents of the religious magazines, usually under their initials only. Many were written for the use of Sunday-schools, the bad versifier's haven at the end of the eighteenth century. Let a single example suffice:

> *While vice, the world's wide spreading flood,*
> *Had filled the good with fear;*
> *Lo! sovereign mercy stood prepared*
> *To wipe the swelling tear.*[14]

In spite of such rubbish, the Evangelicals, in their adoption of Watts, and in the person of Charles Wesley, provided a heritage of children's hymns which survives in some measure to this day.

The importance of Prayer was stressed by the Evangelicals. So important did they believe it, indeed, that it is possible that an overstress on the efficacy of prayer led in part to the evangelical love of special providences. Isaac Milner stressed its importance when he wrote to a dying boy that most of his blessings came from his father's prayers: ' ... how wonderfully Almighty God has blessed him in his children. The explanation is, he is a praying father, and God is a hearer of prayer'.[15]

It was essential, therefore, that children should learn to pray early, but the form of prayer was left in the main— perhaps wisely—to parents.

The few examples we have of prayers written especially for children are not happy ones. Even the example of Dr Watts was not helpful. His 'Morning Prayer for an Infant at three or four years old' begins, 'Almighty God, the Maker of everything in Heaven or Earth ...', a prayer equally suitable at five or fifteen or fifty, though his prayers for children from four to eight and from five to ten and so on (arbitrary divisions, surely) are proportionately more difficult.

The earliest in time were John Wesley's prayers, but again they might well have been written for adults, and they scarcely seem evangelical.

No more apparently evangelical is the prayer book of Stonhouse; most of the prayers are very formal, very close to the prayer book, and borrowed from Bishop Gibson or Dr Watts. The evangelical savour is only sensed in occasional phrasings—'I desire with all seriousness and reverence to look up to thee'.

More evangelical in tone is Rowland Hill's 'Prayer for a Child' when the 'Heart is broken for sin', and Stonhouse's own strange treatise on *Ejaculatory Prayers*. In this union of Puritan and Evangelical, we are told such prayers 'may be exercised at any time.... Every sentence of the Lord's Prayer may be considered ... if it suits our particular case'. Moreover, 'we should endeavour therefore to read the Word of God carefully ... then we shall never want suitable Ejaculations, never be at a loss for expressions to carry on a correspondence with heaven....' That children followed this advice many death-bed accounts prove.

The charnel-house aspect of evangelical teaching for children can be found in Hanway's children's prayer 'For a happy death', while a similar tradition (in this case almost certainly Puritan) is found in the lines:

> *I go to bed as to my grave,*
> *And pray to God my life to save ...*

which were sung to Adam Clarke by his mother.

Before turning to the Evangelicals' contribution to writings for children, it is necessary to consider

CHILDREN'S BOOKS IN THE EIGHTEENTH CENTURY

The most popular reading for children in an age when children were considered only as young adults was whatever the adults read. If the adults were of the fashionable kind, therefore, the children could read Fielding, Smollett, Sterne, and Richardson, all abridged 'for the amusement of youth'; though it is difficult to imagine what would be left of Smollett if his works were seriously abridged, how the insidious obscenity of Sterne would be eradicated, or how abridgement would lessen the unpleasantness of the protracted rape which is 'Pamela'.

If the parents were semi-illiterate (or even illiterate, since chap-books had woodcuts) then the children would read chap-books. These were pamphlets illustrated by crude, and often obscene, wood-cuts, their subjects being marvels, horror stories, crimes, pseudo-religious miracles, and coarse jokes. The latter type, called Jest-books, were too foul to be reproduced by the chronicler of the subject,[16] yet such writings were the only reading of the vast majority of the English during the eighteenth century.

Chap-books were rarely written especially for children; it was assumed that the whole family would read them. One of the exceptions makes no deviation from the common pattern. This is the *Bloody Tragedy, or a Dreadful Warning to Disobedient Children!*[17] It tells how John Gill slits his parents' throats, ravishes the maid and kills her, sets the house on fire after robbing it, is haunted by the ghosts of the dead bodies, and finally makes a dying speech to warn children before his execution.

In secular literature for children—which the Evangelicals usually opposed—great strides were made through the work of the publisher John Newbery, who between 1740 and 1767 published for children a host of books which were decent, moral, and vigorous, while almost the only survivors of an earlier age were Defoe's *Robinson Crusoe* (1719) (if this can be called a secular book) and Swift's *Gulliver's Travels* (1726) in its abridged form.

It was outside these trends that the Evangelicals wrote until at the turn of the nineteenth century, the two streams merged, and the 'moral tale' became common to both traditions.

There was a general dislike of fairy stories during the period and such different people as Goldsmith, Rousseau, Maria Edgworth and Mrs Trimmer opposed them vehemently. Adam Clarke alone defended them.

Easily the most important religious book for children was Bunyan's *Pilgrim's Progress*, acclaimed by all parties. Later, and in a similar tradition was *A Little Book for Little Children* by Thomas White, which contained the cheering advice: 'Read also often Treatises of Death, and Hell, and Judgement, and the Love and Passion of Christ'.

The greatest influence in evangelical circles, however, was not *Pilgrim's Progress*, though it was highly valued, but

Janeway's *A Token for Children*. It would be difficult to exaggerate the importance of this book for the Evangelicals. Scores of works were written in imitation of it, scores of happy deaths attributed to its influence, and it was regarded as the standard reading for children of evangelical parents. Wesley not only recommended it but published an edition himself.

We turn, therefore, to this much-loved masterpiece for children, wondering what excellences it has to commend itself for more than a hundred years.

The Preface is addressed 'To all Parents, School-Masters and School-Mistresses'. The author assures them he 'knew a child that was converted by this sentence, from a godly schoolmistress in the country: 'Every mother's child of you are by nature children of wrath'.

A second Preface for children begins, 'You may now hear, my dear lambs . . .'. Janeway briefly recommends heaven, and then gets down to the real business of his work, which is to terrify children into pious paths.

'Are you willing to go to hell, to be burned with the devil and his angels? . . . O! Hell is a terrible place. . . . Did you never hear of a little child that died . . . and if other children die, why may not you be sick and die? . . . How do you know but that you may be the next child that may die? . . . Now tell me, my pretty dear child, what will you do? . . .'

The kernel of the book consists of thirteen accounts, in two parts, of the pious deaths of children, most of them under ten, some as young as two, all utterly certain of heaven. Were there not dozens of similar accounts of pious deaths for more than a hundred years afterwards, the accounts would be incredible. We read of a child who, between two and three years old, 'when he was at secret prayer wept bitterly', of a girl between five and six whose 'business was to be reading, praying, discoursing about the things of God . . .', of another between four and five who was 'very solicitous about her soul and her everlasting condition', of another four-year-old who told other children they should not laugh 'till you have grace', and of the infinitely pathetic dying boy of seven who said, thinking of his precious toys: 'Away with all the pleasant things in the world; away with my dagger!'

That many people were suspicious of these accounts is proven by Janeway's Preface to the second work, where he quotes the doubts that had been raised but defends the veracity of the accounts.

Hagiographers of all ages have been puzzled by child saints, but it takes a very confirmed cynic to laugh at it all. The Evangelicals did not laugh. Doubts never crossed their minds, and it is interesting to speculate how many evangelical children died piously through the influence of Janeway.

EVANGELICAL BOOKS FOR CHILDREN

Wesley's *Lessons for Children* and *Instructions for Children* have already been considered in Chapter 2. Little mention, however, has been made of the great importance of his Bookroom in spreading popular literature. Through his insistence on the Itinerants hawking Methodist publications wherever they went, Wesley's influence on popular education was enormous. 'In this manner', says Thomas Jackson, 'a taste for reading was created in families, and profitable books supplanted profane conversation and sports on the Lord's Day. Useful knowledge was diffused, and especially on the all-important subject of true religion.'[18]

More in the tradition of Janeway was Whitefield's *The Life of Emelia Geddie . . . from her Infancy to her Death . . . Recommended to the Young Ones Especially*, which recounts the pious death of poor Emelia. She died in 1688, was used later in George Burder's book of pious deaths, and thereafter appears regularly.

John Crosse also published 'several easy little books', including *An Attempt to assist Youth in the great and important work of Religion*, which contains the compelling blurb: 'As you would escape the perpetual gnawing of the never dying worm, and the extreme torture of the unquenchable flame, read this little book over and over again.'[19]

There was an underlying feeling among Evangelicals that the only book that children should read was the Bible. Hence little was written for them at the beginning of the Evangelical Revival. Towards the end of the century, however, this belief was not held by the second generation, and the 'moral tale' had its vogue.

An interesting example of a bridge between the Janeway tradition (which survived at least to the middle of the nineteenth century) and the new style is the Rev. George Burder's *Early Piety, or Memoirs of Children Eminently Religious*. We are introduced to 'Master Billy and Miss Betsy Goodchild', who are under the care of 'Mrs Lovegood'. She, 'a lady of singular piety and wisdom', rewards the children for remembering sermons well with 'some useful information that was new to them'. We are not surprised that they are a 'happy because pious family'.

The second chapter is an allegorical maze, with several borrowings from Bunyan, while the third tells of a visit to the museum (the keeper is 'a venerable minister') where a picture of Vesuvius erupting, naturally reminds Billy of the day of judgement. However, 'nothing pleased Master Goodchild more than an old MS of the Bible on vellum'.

Chapter 4 begins at a children's party, where the company can think of no better way of passing the time than in each telling 'some pretty history which they had read, that might tend to their mutual advantage'. The 'pretty histories' are pious deaths, the miserable death of a wicked child (Elisha's bald head pops up briefly that children may be devoured by bears), and an account of conversions at Whitefield's Orphan-House.

Chapter 9, on 'God's Providence', is an even more confusing allegory than Chapter 2. A strange man steals a gold cup, gives it to a miser, breaks a baby's neck, and then pushes his guide into a river and drowns him. Then he changes into an angel, and explains his fantastic conduct by even more fantastic quixotry. (He killed the child because it had 'almost weaned his affections from God'.)

This dreadful work ends with a 'Sermon on the Pleasures of Religion'. Such stuff might well make children hypocrites or madmen. Every pious cliché, every tasteless and frightening device is dragged in, and the spirits of Bunyan, and Watts and Whitefield gloom down on a man who, like Sir Fretful Plagiary, could not even steal with taste.

Typical of the later 'moral' school is Hanway, whose rather nauseous style recounts how Richard Ramble returns a shilling, which had been given him in error, to the Squire. That worthy 'took occasion . . . to present him to them as . . . an honest good little boy: they made a circle round him. Among the rest was Harry Heart-good, a remarkably good-minded boy: Harry had but one poor $\frac{1}{2}$d. in the world, but he was so affected with the account given of Dick's honesty, as a friend to virtue, and to virtue's friends, he stepped forward and presented Dick with this piece of money . . .'[20]

In part Rowland Hill's work for children, *Instructions for Children, or, a Token of Love for the Rising Generation*, was in the full Janeway tradition. His section on 'Lives and Deaths of Good Children' closely rivals his great predecessor in this field. On one occasion he even enters heaven to make sure of a safe arrival: '. . . She expired in rapture of holy triumph; and was taken by angels to dwell for ever with the Lord.' In part Hill attempted to do what Wesley had tried before him, to make theology simple for children. Yet he does not succeed. 'Adam and Eve never wanted clothing till they lost their innocence, and then they found themselves naked to their shame; so that the very cloaths we wear prove us to be sinners before God'; this is hardly clear. Throughout his work Rowland Hill seems to doubt if he should have written it at all. 'I meant at first', he says apologetically, 'to prove to poor children the sinfulness of their hearts; if we have been a little prevented by some alluring stories, we will now proceed.'

Hannah More is more easily considered under 'Tracts', but her sister author, Mrs Trimmer, not an Evangelical but much respected by them, achieved enormous popularity and esteem by her *Fabulous Histories*. It was a highly 'moral' book, tediously so by modern standards, and its aim was to teach children goodness through stories from nature. Her regard for veracity was so remarkable that, having introduced a 'mock bird' into her very English story, she gravely added the footnote; 'The mock bird is properly a native of America, but is introduced here for the sake of the moral.'[21] It was also this good lady who took such exception to fairy tales, and *Cinderella* in particular, since it 'paints the worst passions that can enter the human heart ... such as envy, jealousy, a dislike to mother-in-law and half-sisters, vanity ...'. None of her work was religious in the full evangelical sense, and her wordy style was hardly, as she claimed in the Preface, 'adapted to the comprehension of young persons'.

The Dairyman's Daughter, by Legh Richmond, had a very considerable vogue among adults as well as among children. Judged by our standards it is a mawkish piece. An evangelical Parson is sent for by the dairyman's daughter, who is dying of consumption. Ostensibly she seeks his ghostly advice, but in fact she dispenses it—at wearisome length. All the evangelical clichés are trotted out by the girl ('washed in the blood of the lamb', 'begged me to flee from the wrath to come'), and the Parson provides an obligato of cadaverous approval. He commends in a funeral the 'impressive tendency of our truly evangelical Liturgy', and we learn that on this happy occasion one reprobate had a conviction of sin and was saved.

Her death is grisly in the extreme, long, painful, and punctuated by pious monologues. It is the crux of the book, and Legh Richmond is certainly in the Janeway tradition. It differs from Janeway in its elaboration and in its inexpert attempt to connect the story (though it is fact, not fiction) to the pious death. One element which came in with the 'moral' tale was a stress on the blessings of poverty, and the element is present here. The predominant element, however, is the charnel-house, and Richmond emphasizes this to the last by the recital of the girl's will, in which she chooses her own funeral hymns, including Charles Wesley's most gruesome

> *Ah lovely appearance of death!*
> *No sight upon earth is so fair!*
> *Not all the gay pageants that breathe,*
> *Can with a dead body compare:*
> *With solemn delight I survey*
> *The corpse when the spirit is fled,*
> *In love with the beautiful clay,*
> *And longing to lie in its stead.*[22]

Legh Richmond also wrote *The Negro Servant*, *The Young Cottager*, *The Cottage Conversation*, and *A Visit to the Infirmary*. Each title suggests the nature of the work.

We get a fair idea of Richmond as a teacher from the second of these books. He meets a group of twelve-year-olds in his churchyard—a home from home for a man of his temperament. 'I had not far to look for subjects of warning and exhortation suitable to my little flock of lambs that I was feeding—I could point to the heaving sods that marked the different graves ... and tell my pupils that you are as they were, none of them were too young to die ... and that probably more than half of the bodies which were buried there, were those of little children.' He then made his pupils learn the texts on the tombs by heart.

Another book which found favour among the later Evangelicals (Dr Coke had a large number of copies printed for circulation) was the account by a child of the deaths of her two younger brothers. This also is pure Janeway, though the childish style of writing gives it a macabre piquancy all its own.[23]

Easily the most famous writer for children of this period was Mrs Sherwood. Her great book, *The Fairchild Family*, was not published until 1848, but it was the culmination of a school of writing, and must be considered in that light. Mrs Sherwood was a Church of England Calvinist. Her evangelical solidity may be judged by her comments on her father: 'I do not think that his ideas of doctrine were ever clearly defined; neither he nor my mother had any distinct ideas of human depravity'.[24] Mrs Sherwood, however, had. She was decided in all her ways, and she was a great authority on bringing up children. One marvels to read how, while touring with her children in Lyons, she closed the blinds of her hotel window to protect them from the sight of a fun fair, and preached to them instead.[25]

Such a woman might well write with fierce determination, nor can we read much of her *Fairchild Family* without an appalled pity for the children who were subjected to such a régime. The famous 'Blackwood' passage, a masterpiece of the macabre, ends with these children being confronted by 'a gibbet, on which the body of a man hung in chains ... but the face of the corpse was so shocking, that the children could not look upon it'. This is bad enough, but there is a considerably worse passage in which the children (ages six to twelve) visit the putrefying corpse of a neighbour. The detailed description makes even a strong stomach quail. The reason for the Blackwood visit was a quarrel over a doll; the rotting corpse had murdered his brother. The reason for the second was Mrs Fairchild's question, apropos of nothing whatever: 'Have you ever seen a corpse, my dears?' Yet disgusting as this may be, the real horror of it all, the blasphemy of the book, is that Mr Fairchild seems to think he is God. It is impossible for him to do wrong, and the children live in the shadow of his terrifying omniscience. When the grosser horrors are dissolved in uneasy laughter, still this remains.

Like Wesley, Mrs Sherwood assembled school books, interpolating passages of Scripture to leaven the lump of information that passed for a school text-book in those days. But these, beside the *Fairchild Family*, were trivial. *The Fairchild Family* was, in a sense, the last great Puritan work for children. Its sale was enormous, its influence incalculable, and the measure of its success was the rapture with which it was received. At last England knew how children were to be brought up! At last children could read, in exciting story form, how they should behave! And the later Evangelicals knew that their children were safe from harm; there was Mrs Sherwood to read and, if that ever palled, there was always *Wet Sunday Afternoons with Joshua*.[26]

TRACTS

The distinction between a tract and a book is a fine one, and the division would appear arbitrary. It is not arbitrary for two reasons. In the first place, the purpose of a tract differs in that its author is, generally speaking, irrelevant. Its purpose is to disseminate religious knowledge to as wide an audience as possible, and the price is kept as low as possible that this may be done. In the second place, the historical importance of the cheap *Repository Tracts* by Hannah More is so great that this alone justifies the division.

It is necessary first to consider briefly early eighteenth-century tracts in order to compare them with those by Evangelicals. They can be divided into various types. A number were plainly of Church origin, and were designed to help serious Christian children. They made little, if any, attempt to meet the real needs of children, but quoted the Church's authority on such matters in a far-from-simple style. Another type was written for the use of school-children, but here again they might as easily have been written for adults. A third type, more interesting from its apparently evangelical viewpoint, concerned pious lives of children, while another type, closely related, gives accounts of pious children of the past. The latter types are not as evangelical as they sound; they are historical accounts, not in a style particularly applicable to children, and could equally well have been written by a devout High Church-man, a Puritan, or an Evangelical.

For purposes of comparison we turn abruptly to two evangelical tracts, very different in character, but each, had the authorship been unknown, would have been pronounced emphatically the work of an Evangelical.

The first is by Newton and seems, but only seems, to be a typical pious death in the Janeway tradition: *A Monument to the Praise of the Lord's Goodness, and to the memory of dear Eliza Cuningham.* The child was Newton's adopted niece, and it reveals, albeit unconsciously, since there is not a hint of pride throughout, Newton's own amazing courage in her death. Here are no pious clichés, no glib claims of a special providence of God, only a movingly simple certainty of heaven for a child who died more certain of the world to come than the world she left. Typically evangelical are the thoughts that this world did not matter, that heaven was the only attainment that counted, that an apparently pure life was no way to salvation, and that only a second birth could make death, not merely acceptable, but a triumphant joy.

The second tract is quite as evangelical in tone yet, lacking the personal experience which gave birth to the first, and coming also from a harder, more puritanical source, it repels as much as the first attracts: Burder's *Serious Address to Sick Persons, and not only to persons in dying circumstances, but to all others who are ignorant of the Great Salvation.* This tract finds the near approach of death a justification for extreme use of terror. 'The most awful, the most tremendous sight the sun beholds, from rising morn till the cool shadows of evening take place, is an immortal soul just bidding adieu to a perishing body ... ignorant of God ... the grave just opening to receive his body: devils spreading their black wings around his bed.' And later, this poor soul must go 'into the presence of an incensed Judge, a just and jealous God, whose thunderbolts of vengeance shall drive every sinner ...'. Whatever one thinks about the substance of Burder's theme, or the appropriateness of it all, one must admit it is well done. This work, unlike the tracts of the early eighteenth century, appeals to the emotions. It calls for the heart religion which the Evangelicals demanded. If it is coarse in its appeal, and crude in its theology, it is still effective. Unlike the earlier tracts, it forces a line of conduct.

Hannah More, the old Bishop in Petticoats, as William Cobbett so aptly called her, was a mass of contradictions. She never knew enough theology to be sure what Calvinism meant, yet she indulged in theological writings; she was methodistic, yet openly opposed the Methodists; she mixed with the great freely, and opposed nearly all their ways in her writings; and she attacked secular writings for children and then devoted her life to producing them. In addition to all this, or in spite of it, she was a very clever woman, in some ways far ahead of her times.

While a child herself she wrote 'supposititious letters to depraved characters, intended to reclaim them'[27] and this early habit she never outgrew. Indeed, it became her life's work, and nowhere was she more successful than in her cheap *Repository Tracts*. Initially, they appear to have been written against the revolutionary tendencies which the works of Paine had roused, but Hannah More was too much an Evangelical to feel that there was any answer to revolution except vital religion. 'Dry morality or religion', she wrote, 'will not answer the end, for we must ever bear in mind that it is a pleasant poison to which we must find an antidote.'[28]

The tracts, published anonymously, were written and composed with consummate skill. Not only were most of them written in a bold, simple, vigorous style, not only were the stories good in their own right as well as being pointedly moral, but even their appearance was clever; they looked exactly like the bawdy chap-books which hawkers sold throughout England.

The sales were fabulous. In 1795, 300,000 copies were sold in six weeks, and one cannot doubt that the circulation far exceeded this. The influence remained throughout the first half of the nineteenth century, and in 1866 Colquhoun was able to write that the great improvement in religion and morals of the preceding twenty years was owing chiefly 'to Robert Raikes's Sunday-schools and to Hannah More's writings'.[29]

Curiously enough, though nearly all England rang with Hannah More's praises on her achievement, a number of her evangelical companions were doubtful about her venture. The *Evangelical Magazine*, which in 1795 had warmly applauded the idea of the circulation 'of religious and useful knowledge, as an antidote to the poison continually flowing through the channel of those licentious publications which are vended about our cities', and in 1797, in an article entitled 'Information Requested on the Means of Doing Good' urged the appointing of 'some general Repository in the Metropolis', reviewed Hannah More's tracts the same year in a very lukewarm way: 'The narrative pieces are well calculated to excite the attention of children and un-educated persons to useful instruction. We would recommend, as much as possible, the adoption of real facts on the ground of these little histories; as we think that danger of some kind usually lurks beneath the flowers of fiction.' Poor Hannah More.

Her 'flowers of fiction' had other elements which some Evangelicals might have disliked. For instance, there is no stress on personal conversion, and this had always been the centre of evangelical theology. Further, the vast majority of her characters are good or bad, apparently from birth. Where is the saving grace that makes even the vilest sinner a child of God? And Hannah More could also see the dangers of her own creed. While *The Touchstone* attacks 'the merely nominal and false Christians' it also attacks the group who 'are very remarkable for their attachment to certain Christian doctrines, and are very zealous for what they call the Gospel', yet 'are ready to turn away from what they call so merely moral a lesson' (the example of Christ). How dangerous! Nor was this all. In *The Black Prince, a True Story*, we read that he 'was not a Christian, but who was a better man (to their shame be it spoken) than many who call themselves Christians'.

There was a variety of cheap *Repository Tracts*. Some, such as *The Fall of Adam* and *Noah's Flood*, were attempts to make the Scriptures clearer and easier and also, of course, gave an evangelical interpretation to such important doctrines as the first of these. Another type was less scriptural in one sense, though based on texts; *The General Resurrection* is an example of such. Yet another is represented by *Explanation of the Nature of Baptism* (possibly written by Zachary Macaulay, one of Hannah More's Clapham Sect friends), a church-centred tract.

The most popular, however, were the less religious stories which sweetened the pill of instruction with the sugar of a tale of woe, for preference with a happy ending. Such was *Betty Brown: A St Giles' Orange Girl, with some account of Mrs Sponge, the Money-Lender*. It is a pity that Hannah More, having told a fascinating tale of London life, and of virtue triumphing over adversity, had to end with a dull *Rules for Retail Dealers*, but Dickens himself, whom Hannah More in some ways anticipated, could not resist moral indignation at social injustice, even at the cost of spoiling a good story.

Not all the stories could have happy endings. *The Cheapside Apprentice*, for example, tells his own miserable story which is to end at Tyburn, but there are compensations in misery. It is no unpleasing thing to wallow in grief, and Hannah More knew this well. *The Good Mother's Legacy* is the horrible story of a bad daughter ('our butler at length betrayed me to ruin') who returns home with her bastard child, gets lost, and both are found dying in the snow. Betty Adams 'tried to speak, but in vain: a ghostly hue overspread her features, her limbs shivered, her jaws fell, and with a deep groan, she expired'.

No opportunity of propaganda is missed. In *The History of Hester Wilmot* poor parents are advised not to 'fall into that sad mistake, that because their children are poor, and have little of this world's goods, the mothers must make it up to them in false indulgence. The children of the gentry are much more reproved and corrected for their faults, and bred up in far stricter discipline.' The shade of Susanna Wesley haunts the second and third generation.

But other elements are here. If Hannah More found it her 'Christian duty to persuade children of the absolute claims of religion', it is pleasant—and surprising—to remember that Marianne Thornton said of her: 'Good woman as she was, she taught me to believe in Tom Thumb nearly as implicitly as in Joseph and his brethren.'[30]

PICTURES

Pictures were rarely used by the Evangelicals as a means of teaching religion. Primarily it was a question of cost. How dear good illustrations were is shown by Mrs Trimmer's *Family Magazine*. Each copy (1788–9) contains one excellent picture, but the magazine cost three shillings per issue. The few examples we possess, therefore, are characterized by the needs of economy; they are crude. Many are woodcuts, which in some cases, judging by the evidence of clothes, and so on, had been made many years before, and were only borrowed by the Evangelicals.

Janeway's example was a poor one. Some of his editions appeared with very bad woodcuts arranged haphazardly through the book. This example, however, hardly excuses the illustrations in Wright's *Spiritual Songs for Children* (1796), where the woodcuts are so bad that it is impossible in most cases to tell what they illustrate. Two consecutive whole-page illustrations, 'On the Day of Judgement' and 'Remember your Creator', look the same. Another picture entitled 'A Wedding Song' shows a jester holding a flag in one hand and a basket containing a dog in the other. The jester is riding a hobby horse and beside him is an angel covering his face with his hands. It is all very strange.

George Burder's illustrations in *Early Piety*, villainously executed, contrast with those in Rowland Hill's *Instructions for Children*; the former illustrates the less religious aspects of his writing, while the latter daringly—and hideously—illustrates the more religious. The latter are therefore more interesting.

Hill commends his illustrations in the Preface, assuring children, who had already seen the first one, that 'not only that picture, but some more are to be found in this little book, that children may be both pleased and profited while they read'. The picture already approved by the child mind shows two stiff, ethereal parents gazing into eternity, each holding an open book, while five apparently half-witted children—three girls and two boys—dressed for outdoors, stand round them. Here is the ideal for family worship.

The second picture shows a pulpited preacher surrounded by children, while the third, a man feeding a horse, appears to illustrate the author feeding a lamb. This curiosity is explained by close scrutiny of the text: the picture is merely out of place. The fourth, to illustrate 'all liars shall have their part in the lake which burneth with fire and brimstone', depicts devils in hell fire, but it is not really as terrifying as Hill might have desired.

After the section on 'good children' a picture shows a little girl being carried to heaven by an angel. Both the child and the angel have remarkably inappropriate expressions; the child appears reluctant, the angel leers horribly. No doubt the possession of pictures was itself a keen pleasure; children would not complain at the lack of artistry.

The charnel-house element in religious instruction was demonstrated in pictures also, and we find them surviving as late as 1827, when woodcuts from the previous century were used to illustrate the anonymous *Poetry for Young Persons*. Of the nine woodcuts, three show graveyards, one a death-bed, and one a dying orphan.

The cleverest use of illustrations was by Hannah More, who, as already mentioned, published her tracts in imitation of the chap-books, and so used similar pictures. Possibly part of the unsympathetic review in the *Evangelical Maga-*

zine, mentioned above, was directed at the illustrations. The picture for the 'Honest Publican', for instance (four figures by an ale-house), proves a knowledge of the world in every line of it.

DRAMA

Since the Theatre was anathema to them, it is astonishing that Evangelicals wrote plays at all. After the turn of the century it became fairly common, but the only drama up to 1800 by an Evangelical is Hannah More's 'The Search after Happiness'. It is not typical of her, it cannot be called evangelical in any normal sense, and it is only interesting as a rarity. A very stupid one, the play was written for girls at boarding-schools, and it told how 'four young ladies of distinction' turned from Pleasure, Languor, Guilt, Excess, and dull Satiety:

> *Where dissipation wears the name of Bliss:*
> *From these we fly in search of Happiness.*

Finally, Urania, a Matron of the piece, presumably to be played by the Headmistress, brings the drama to a climax with the sole mention of Christianity.

> *Then look no more abroad: in your own breast*
> *Seek the true seat of happiness and rest.*
> *Nor small, my friends, the vigilance I ask:*
> *Watch well yourselves: this is the Christian's task.*

Follow three couplets, all bad rhymes, and another hint, but only a hint, of Christianity.

POETRY

The Puritans wrote poetry for children, but not all of it would be considered suitable today. John Marchant, for instance, included in his *Lusus Juveniles* a poem entitled 'Decoy Ducks; or the Pleasures of a Brothel'. The tradition of the Evangelicals lies not so much, however, with the Puritans in general, as with the poetry of Isaac Watts in particular, just as it did with his hymns. 'Verse', he says, in the Preface to his poems, 'was at first designed for the service of God, though it hath been wretchedly abused since. ... So that you will find here nothing that savours of a party.' The Evangelicals, therefore, were free to adopt him, though they were less successful than Watts when they 'endeavoured to sink the language to the level of a child's understanding, and yet to keep it, if possible, above contempt'.

None could match his beautiful 'Cradle Hymn':

> *Lo, he slumbers in his manger,*
> *Where the hornèd oxen fed:*
> *Peace, my darling, here's no danger,*
> *Here's no ox a-near thy bed;*

nor write anything so worthy of parody as:

> *'Tis the voice of the sluggard: I hear him complain,*
> *'You have wak'd me too soon, I must slumber again!'—*

but all approved, and some emulated, his subjects, such as 'The Thief' and 'Good Resolutions', though 'Innocent Play' would have pleased some but offended others. The Wesleys, at least, would have found this last title a contradiction in terms.

Rowland Hill, though he tried to imitate Watts in his 'Sonnet of Instruction', was unsuccessful, and the unhappy women poets of the *Arminian Magazine* and *Evangelical Magazine* (such as 'Serena' and 'Eliza') were even worse. J. Wright wrote his *Spiritual Songs* allegedly for children, but they are unsuitable both in style and content for their intended audience. 'An Elegy upon the sudden death of my very loving and much lamented friend, Mr Nicholas Chamberlain', in heroic couplets, seems poor fare.

Child poets were fairly common, but they usually left their effusions to be found after death, and their subjects were usually morbid.

P.S.—5

I see a hand you cannot see,
That beckons me away:
I hear a voice you cannot hear
That says, I must not stay.[31]

We wait for Hannah More to marshal her muse into action. Her *Sacred Dramas*, dull poetry for refined young ladies, is best forgotten. The poetry of her tracts is more important. Her verse was doggerel, but at least it was exciting doggerel, and it would certainly appeal to children.

It varies from the humorous,

A Tale I tell whose first beginning
May set some giddy folks a grinning
(JOHN THE SHOP-KEEPER),

to the horrible;

Till Molly and Molly's poor baby were found
One evening in Richard's own mill-pond both drowned
(ROBERT AND RICHARD, OR THE GHOST OF POOR MOLLY),

and she always thumps home her moral message. For instance, the man who is to die on the gallows begins his life of crime very early:

In early life with petty thefts
His course he did begin
(THE EXECUTION OF WILD ROBERT: A WARNING TO PARENTS);

and when, at his execution, his Mother interrupts the proceedings to beg a last kiss, he refuses:

You gave me life, but with it gave,
What made that life a curse:
My sins uncurbed, my mind untaught,
Soon grew from bad to worse.

Hannah More understood children.

MAGAZINES

No magazines were published exclusively for children during the eighteenth century, but most evangelical publications remembered the young.

The earliest important publication was the *Gospel Magazine* of 1774, that 'unhappy mixture of Bible and Billingsgate', as Dr Henry Bett called it, a high Calvinist periodical whose main purpose was to blister Arminians. It took little account of children. The Arminians' reply, published by Wesley four years later as *The Arminian Magazine*, was less acid, but at first made its chief aim denunciation of Calvinists. It did, however, remember the needs of young Arminians in a limited way; accounts of Kingswood School, pious deaths of children, and articles on the importance of religious education were all for children, directly or indirectly. Certainly children read the magazines, for Thomas Jackson records: 'My Father resolved that each of his children should have a volume of this periodical bound in calf.'[32]

The *Theological Miscellany*, started in 1784, had virtually nothing for children, but the short-lived *Family Magazine* of 1788 was as much for children as for adults. Its name was justified. It had a long-winded sub-title, *A Repository of Religious Instruction, and rational Amusement, designed to counteract the pernicious Tendency of immoral Books, etc., which have circulated of late years among the inferior classes of People to the obstruction of their improvement in Religion and Morality.* Mrs Trimmer, whose project the magazine was, was not an Evangelical, and the work is that of a Moralist. Nevertheless, the presence of articles on 'Sunday Employment', the stories of sudden Reformations, and the inclusion of hymns and poems (though one of the latter is 'Black Ey'd Susan') show how alike the propaganda of Orthodox and Evangelical Churchmen (or at any rate those of the School of Hannah More) was becoming. Once the Evangelicals had seemed the only serious Christians; now the High Churchmen had rallied, the Evangelicals had lost some of their earlier single-mindedness, and both had met towards the end of the century in a movement which seemed more morality than religion, and, ironically, more works than faith.

In 1793 the *Evangelical Magazine* came into being, and it was probably this that Charlotte Brontë had in mind when she wrote of 'mad Methodist Magazines full of miracles and apparitions and preternatural warnings, ominous dreams, and frenzied fanaticisms'.[33] This magazine aimed a number of articles at children. 'A Caution to Youth', 'Cautions to the Young not to Presume on Long Life', and 'A Word to the Young' are typical.[34] The latter gets straight to the point. 'My dear brethren and sisters! My soul longs for your salvation! What can I do to promote it? ... Remember, the eye of God is ever upon you. Think much of death, of judgement, and eternity.'

Nor was it only such passages as these that children were expected to read. They were expected to read it all. The preface to the 1793 edition explains that 'The subjects ... are calculated to please as well as to instruct, that the children of religious parents, whose interests deserve particular attention, may be allowed, through pleasure, into the paths of true wisdom. Biography, Memoirs, Diaries, Authentic Anecdotes, Striking Providences, and the Expressions of Dying Christians, arrest the mind of the reader and make a deep impression'. And so the infant reader could go on and be edified by a Life of John Berridge, an essay on Ecclesiastical History, and 'A Funeral Meditation'.

And they did. We read of Margaret Graeme, who died at thirteen; she 'had been a constant reader of the Evangelical Magazine since its commencement. It is amazing, now when it recurs to our mind, with what eagerness and fixed attention she read the Obituaries: and with what innocence and unaffected gravity she would wish her experience and last end might be like many of those to which we would refer'.[35] She had her wish.

If this seems remarkable, there is a more astonishing case, that of a child of six who, dying, asked her sister to read an account from the magazine of a Mrs Chase. 'Read it to me, sister,' she said. 'Read where she is dying.'[36]

After death-beds, the speciality of the *Evangelical Magazine* was 'Remarkable Providences' such as 'A remarkable Judgement against a Profane Man' or 'The Wilful

Liar's dreadful appeal'. The worst of these were almost incredibly silly; the best mark the dividing line between the religious man and the sceptic.

DIARIES

A huge number of the Evangelicals wrote diaries. Wesley encouraged it, and especially encouraged children to do so. Few children's diaries, however, survive. Most were presumably destroyed by their owners on reaching maturity, and mature thoughts on their childhoods substituted for the earlier and more interesting ones.

All evangelical diaries are strange ones—they form a pattern peculiar to their own kind—introverted, deeply religious, often tortured, occasionally ecstatic, tending to cliché. All, in spite of being introverted, are somehow self-consciously so, as if the author suspected that man—or God—would take them down and use them in evidence against them.

The most remarkable of all is the *Journal of Mary Gilbert*, first published by Wesley. No editorial hand has improved it, and it is the day-by-day account of a child's own soul. She died at seventeen. The book is at once moving and terrifying. So important is it as a child's own reactions to her religious background that it has been reserved for fuller study in our final Chapter 6.

A consideration of the two most important means of evangelical education, preaching and Sunday-schools, is also reserved. The former is most easily discussed in connexion with the Church and the latter with Schools; They will therefore be examined in the chapter which follows.

REFERENCES

1. Thomas Jackson, *Recollections*, pp. 18–9.
2. W. Morgan, *The Parish Priest*, pp. 89–94.
3. M. Seeley, *Later Evangelical Fathers*, p. 25.
4. Mrs Mary Fletcher, *A Legacy to the People of Madeley*, Preface, *passim.*
5. J. H. Pratt, *Eclectic Notes*, p. 7.

6. E. Sidney, *Life of Sir Richard Hill*, pp. 15–6.
7. From the Preface to the 1779 edition of Wesley's hymn-book.
8. E. B. Castle, *Moral Education in Christian Times*, p. 167.
9. Rev. Thomas Scott, *The Force of Truth*, p. 7.
10. J. H. Pratt, *Eclectic Notes*, p. 262.
11. *Poetical Works*, VI, pp. 441–3.
12. Ibid. p. 378.
13. H. Bett, *The Spirit of Methodism*, p. 177.
14. 'Sung by the children of a Sunday School', *Evangelical Magazine* (1800), p. 131.
15. Mary Milner, *Life of Isaac Milner*, p. 239.
16. John Ashton, *Chapbooks of the eighteenth century*; see Preface.
17. Ibid.
18. Thomas Jackson, *Recollections of my own Life and Times*, ed. Frankland, p. 26.
19. W. Morgan, *The Parish Priest*, pp. 94–6.
20. J. A. Hanway, *A Comprehensive View of Sunday Schools*.
21. Mrs Trimmer, *Fabulous Histories* ... (1815 edn.), II, p. 54.
22. *Poetical Works*, VI, p. 193.
23. *A Precious Testimony for Jesus, in the Experience of Two Children, one of ten, the other of twelve years of Age, who lived very comfortably, and died most joyful, in Christ*, ed. W. Mason.
24. N. Royde-Smith, *The State of Mind of Mrs Sherwood*, p. 32.
25. Ibid. p. 166.
26. Ibid. p. 85.
27. *Cambridge History of English Literature*, XI, pp. 359–60.
28. M. G. Jones, quoted in *Hannah More*, p. 139.
29. J. C. Colquhoun, *Wilberforce, His Friends, and His Times*, p. 122.
30. M. G. Jones, quoted in *Hannah More*, p. 97.
31. *Evangelical Magazine* (1797), p. 478.
32. Thomas Jackson, *Recollections*, p. 25.
33. H. F. Mathews, quoted in *Methodism and the Education of the People*, p. 173.
34. *Evangelical Magazine* (1793), p. 66; (1794), p. 412; (1794), p. 118, respectively.
35. Ibid. (1797), p. 212.
36. Ibid. (1800), p. 124.

CHAPTER IV

The Medium of their Teaching

THE EVANGELICALS taught in three spheres, in the home, in their schools, and in church. These three spheres of influence form natural and simple divisions.

HOME

THE RELIGION OF THE HOME

Evangelicalism was the religion of the home. The importance of 'Parlour Religion', as it was often called, spanned the second half of the eighteenth century. Increasingly it became the recognized medium of religious instruction.

What were the characteristics of a pious home? Though fictional and incidental, and perhaps the more convincing because of it, the characteristics suggested in George Burder's *Early Pity* and in Hannah More's *Coelebs in Search of a Wife* give a clear picture. In each case we have a deeply religious atmosphere, godly conversation, industrious use of time, family prayers twice daily, holy books much in evidence, and a conspicuous absence of such devices of the devil as cards, games, and music (except, obviously, hymns).

Whether or not the children found such an atmosphere stifling would depend, at least in part, on the nature of their parents, but Sidney Smith suggests that strong evangelical surroundings would be difficult under any circumstances.

But if Sidney Smith had doubts, the Evangelicals never did. Their only fear was that they might, through lenience, consign their own children to hell. Rather let them die!

> *I ask as with my parting breath,*
> *To each allotted be*
> *A holy life, or early death;*
> *But which I leave to thee.*[1]

And childhood was a dangerous time. The sooner the child grew into a man the better.

> *Shorten his time for childish play,*
> *From youthful lusts and passions screen,*
> *Nor leave him in the wilds to stray*
> *Of pleasure, vanity, and sin.*[2]

Parents had only themselves to blame if the legions of hell were swollen by their offspring. 'Will it not be a melancholy thought, to reflect, at the close of your days, that you have been promoting the designs of Satan, by bringing up children to be a constant torment to you through life, and then to be plunged into everlasting perdition?'[3]

Prevention is better than cure. The Evangelicals began young, and they began by a daily assertion of God in the Family.

FAMILY WORSHIP

Family Worship soon became the badge of evangelical allegiance. Its importance was considerable. As a witness alone it had enormous effect, and the results on the children survived generations. Delight in it is normal. 'My happiest moments are during Family Worship' and 'It is the pleasantest part of my life'[4] are quite usual tributes to it. Many books commended it, and all Gospel periodicals had articles to support it. It suffered the fate of so much evangelical teaching at the end of the century, being applauded, not for its intrinsic merit alone but for its reforming influence, but it survived even this, and lasted far into the nineteenth century.

Virtually all the Evangelicals observed Family Worship. Their methods varied in detail but much was common. Grimshaw's preparation was to rise at four in summer, five in winter, sing loudly the doxology, spend an hour in private, and then hold his family prayers. Cecil, who found it 'easy to keep up the attention of a congregation in comparison of that of my family', felt the service should be 'short, savoury, simple, plain, tender, heavenly', and to that end let his children read the Scriptures in turn and tried to make them feel 'we are a religious family; how natural it is that we should thus meet together'.[5] So also does William Jay attempt to make his family worship a pleasure by using 'short and significant sentences, bold images, striking incidents, lively descriptions and characters'.[6]

There is an idealized picture of Family Worship in the *Evangelical Magazine* of 1794. It describes how it is held in a 'parlour decently prepared'. When it is over 'the happy servants, cheered and warmed with the aids of devotion, return to their duty, each according to his place', while the family 'sit down to breakfast on the overflowing bounty of God's providence'. The Mistress later takes up her station in the parlour. 'The Bible is laid near, to be referred to as her best friend and director, her richest cordial in trouble, and most faithful monitor in doubtful cases.'

If William Jay really prayed as his works assure us ('Let our sons be as plants grown up in their youth, and our daughters as corner stones, polished after the similitude of a palace');[7] if even George Whitefield, who suffered much from the godly, had to rebuke a Master of a family for tediousness; if G. W. E. Russell faithfully records: 'I remember a very distinct impression on my infant mind that the portions of the Bible which were used at Prayers had no meaning, and that the public reading of the words, without reference to sense, was an act of piety';[8] and if James Lackington and his Master's wife used Family Worship as a theological tilting yard, then we may well wonder how much the children profited from it all.

It is an inescapable fact, however, that however abhorrent some of its aspects may seem to us, Family Worship was loved sufficiently by most of the children for them to observe it in their turn, and so it survived and flourished well into the second half of the nineteenth century.

THE THEORY OF FAMILY RELIGION

The Evangelicals liked to make rules. The very term 'Methodists' proves it. Wesley himself, however, in spite of his sermon on 'Family Religion', where he enjoins 'Instruct your children early, plainly, frequently, and patiently', made no rules for Family Religion simply because he had no family to govern.

If other early Evangelicals had rules for their families, none appears to survive. We get some understanding of the ideal, however, in Charles Wesley's hymns.

> *In Jesus' name behold we meet!*
> *Far from an evil world retreat,*
> *And all its frantic ways.*[9]

Nor does he only consider the ideal. The perplexities of the *pater familias* he knew well. How shall I, he asks,

> *A pattern to my household give,*
> *And as a guardian angel live,*
> *As Jesus' minister?*

It was a difficult problem. And how does he know when to assert his and God's authority, when to show mercy?

> *The opposite extremes I see,*
> *Remissness and severity.*
> *Shall I through indolence supine*
> *Neglect, betray my Charge Divine?*
> *A lion in my house, shall I*
> *My tame inferiors terrify*
> *By fierce tyrannic sway?*[10]

Poor Charles Wesley was noted for his impatience.

Later Evangelicals left many sets of rules. Most of them are obvious enough. An article on 'Family Government' in the *Evangelical Magazine* of 1797 gives rules which would be acceptable almost anywhere, but the very strong stress on being obeyed early and absolutely makes it typically evangelical.

William Hey's theories deserve mention as explaining in part the immense effect evangelical teaching had on future generations. He summoned his family in 1797 when he thought he was dying and urged four thoughts on them. The first was that religion was 'apt to degenerate in serious families', the second was that all the godly should 'avoid family connexions with the world', the third was the necessity of 'Allegiance to the Establishment', and the last was a warning to 'guard against the family breaking up'.[11] These four hints go far to explain the strength of the Evangelicals. When his family could least refuse what he asked, Hey summoned them to guard Evangelicalism for the future.

Venn had an even happier idea for ensuring the future. Dying wishes were good; a voice from the tomb was even better. He advised a widow, worried about her son, 'in the most solemn manner, to write a letter explaining to your son what you mean by real religion, and conclude with earnest entreaties that he would lay this matter to heart. ... This letter I would have you seal up, and write upon it, "To be delivered to Mr —— as soon as I am dead" '.[12] And Venn concludes by saying he intends to do this himself.

DISCIPLINE

Here began Wesley's theory, and the discipline of the Evangelicals has always been famous for its rigour. Yet it is doubtful if it was as rigorous as its reputation. As always, so much depended on the individuals. One man's system of discipline can be, not only acceptable, but positively pleasing to children, while another man using precisely the same system can be detested for it.

Here is a clear example. Wesley, well known for his love of children, even if he failed to understand them, asks his readers not to punish children if they could avoid it. If they *must*, 'You should take the utmost care to avoid the very appearance of passion. Whatever is done should be done with mildness; nay, indeed, with kindness too'. This sounds dangerous psychologically, but probably wise as he intended it. Crooke, not many years later, beat his annoying nephew

Henry for some serious fault and then was overcome by an agony of remorse because, though the beating was very mild, it was done in anger.[13] The theory reached independently by its holders is carried further. Henry Longden, the twentieth child of parents who had buried the first nineteen before he was born, was inevitably spoilt, and determined therefore to see that his own children were not treated with such dangerous leniency. We read of him; 'He had recourse, it is true, to coercive measures, yet always with regret, and not, even when most needful, until he had kneeled down to implore the blessing of God upon the correction he was about to inflict.'[14] Steadily the practice becomes more unpleasant.

In Clayton's hands it reaches its summit of cruelty. 'Correction is an ordinance: to be used with prayer. "Thou shalt beat him with a rod, and shall deliver his soul from hell." I have always delayed correction for a time. Children feel this.'[15]

Towards the end of the eighteenth century the Eclectic Society (a Society formed by evangelical clergymen for discussion of their problems) had an interesting meeting to decide 'What are the first and most Prominent Discoveries of Depravity in Children, and the best methods of counteracting them?'[16] 'Self will' was generally agreed to be the most prominent form of depravity, and again the reactions depend on personality. Abdy sadly but humanly admitted he was too lenient. 'My child', he confessed, 'can put on a look that makes me smile even when I am displeased.' Woodd also preferred gentleness: 'If indulgence has slain its thousands, severity has slain its ten thousands.' Others, however, did not agree. Pratt thought that, of the two extremes, 'Laxity gives more trouble in the issue'. Stillingfleet of Hotham agreed: 'I was under a severe parent: but should have been worse, if under an indulgent one.' Scott went further. He attributed 'the present disorders of Europe' to a 'want of the old plan of discipline'. He assured the company: 'I began with my children when they were in arms: this gave less trouble.' It is also Scott who puts his finger on the difficulty of discipline in godly families: 'A Christian parent finds anger rise, begins to fear, and therefore gives way.'

Two of the members of this Society had views we consider typical of the Evangelicals. Goode argued that 'passion may be seen even at the breast: obstinacy too. My child kept me once for two or three hours before its obstinacy would give way: but I conquered and have had no trouble since'. Most remarkable of all is Pattrick's terrifying boast: 'I contended once a whole night with a child when seven months old. And it has left a permanent effect to this day.' No doubt.

Godly children, of course, would be presumed to thank God and their parents for the punishment. If this seems completely inhuman there are several cases of it actually happening. One such case (quoted in the *Evangelical Magazine* of 1799) shows both child and parent in a curious light. A small girl was promised a beating by her Mother, but the Mother forgot. However, 'the dear child reminded the parent of her breach of promise'. The Mother, one assumes, would forgive her. On the contrary. However, 'we need not remark that upon this occasion, the child was not very rigorously beaten'.

FAMILY LIFE

A brief consideration of the way a typical Evangelical planned his day shows how children fit into the scheme. Henry Venn can speak for himself.

'I am up, one of the first in the house, soon after five o'clock, and when prayer and reading the blessed Word is done, my daughters make their appearance and I teach them till Mrs Venn comes down, at half past eight. Then family prayer begins, which is often very sweet, as my mother's maid, and my own servants, are all, I believe, born of God. The children begin to sing prettily. ...' Venn explains how he is employed after lunch and dinner, and between 6 and 7 p.m. he has 'solemn meditation and walking in my house'.

The children join him again from 7 to 8 for family devotions, to which outsiders are invited. He goes to bed at 10 p.m.[17]

The evangelical influence on children is seen in this account. Not only were they present at least for an hour and a half of prayers, morning and night, not only must they be aware of their father's custom of prowling round the house meditating, but the girls, at least, were taught by their father daily, and we may assume that all they were taught had a strong evangelical flavour.

It happens that one leading Evangelical had godly parents of a pattern very different from his own. Richard Venn, father of Henry, was a High Churchman, a Tory, and an opponent of Whitefield. He was also a very hard disciplinarian. He compelled his daughter to go by night into his church by a path that would force her over a grave filled a few hours before. The idea was to cure her fear of the dark. Similarly, when the child unwisely confessed to a dislike for some particular food, 'he suffered no other food to be brought to table till hunger compelled her to eat it'.[18] This is the sort of discipline which is taken as typical of the Evangelicals. But Evangelicalism is not always like its caricature. Not all introspection, not all single-mindedness, not all religious discipline, and not all morbidity are evangelical prerogatives.

It is interesting that Henry Venn had a problem to solve similar to his father's and he dealt with it very differently. When an old man, he took charge of the three-year-old step-son of his daughter. He cured the child of his fear by telling him a Bible-story in the dark, first with the child on his knee, and then by degrees, farther and farther away.[19] The story has a beautiful sequel. The boy grew up and left religious ways. Finally he came back and told his children hundreds of times that Venn had said to him: 'Remember, little John, if anything would make heaven not heaven to me, it would be the not having you with me there.'

Yet it was this gentle old man who had advised the readers of *The Complete Duty of Man*, to tell their children just how terrible it would be to have God for an enemy just after a storm, to 'carry them to the bed of a brother ... or play-fellow, who is sick and in pain', and 'to rivet this instruction', that health and strength are the gifts of God, when 'a servant, or friend ... is just expired'. It is a strange mixture of terror and gentleness.

Like Fletcher—but not as successfully as he—many Evangelicals tried to make sermons out of everyday occasions. Hervey made his two daughters cut an orange with ornamental and tawdry knives they had been given as presents. They failed, but succeeded with plain but serviceable knives. He pointed the moral: beware of a showy dress and person— utility is real value. Cecil persuaded his small daughter to throw her dearly loved beads in the fire, and a few days later gave her much better ones. It was to teach her faith.

Always, and particularly towards the end of the century, Evangelicals expected charitable deeds by their children. In 1798 and 1799, for instance, years of unusual hardship in England, Adam Clarke took his children to see the hungry, ill-clothed waifs about them, and his family voluntarily set aside portions of their own food at every meal. So they were taught true charity—not as a proof of social superiority— but a practical application of the Christian life.

Respect for parents was deep in the evangelical home system. 'A man must be both Priest and King in his family, and Prophet too,' said Goode.[20] This reads uncomfortably like Newton's own hymn:

> *Jesus! my Shepherd, Husband, Friend,*
> *My Prophet, Priest, and King;*

and suggests what has already been noted with reference to the 'Fairchild Family', that the Evangelicals, in relation to their children, were dangerously near identifying themselves with God. In fact at this period the patriarchal theory of family life was common. It was not only the Evangelicals who based their theories on Abraham's system. It would appear that most families worked that way implicitly, without reference to Scripture. The Evangelicals, on the other hand, invariably sought Scriptural authority for their actions, and so it was in the Old Testament that they rested, prepared of course, to add St Paul's words, 'Children, be subject to your Parents', to the weight of Abraham's example. In most cases, fortunately, innate humility left an assumption of God's authority only as a snare to be avoided, but the rights of parents were a continual theme—the unexpressed but deeply held conviction of the 'Divine Right of Parents'.

God's wrath on disobedient children (see Watts's hymn on the subject) was announced in most infant books, and sermons on the fifth commandment were common. Venn systematized it. His first rule was 'to honour them by respectful language: by abstaining from every thing that may reasonably give them the least offence or disquiet', his second, 'to conceal and extenuate the imperfections of their parents, so far as truth and justice will admit'.[21] What irreverent thoughts such a rule conjures up!

Scattered hints reveal to us most clearly how respect for parents was fostered. Hanway not only approves but recommends the old custom of a child falling on his knees to ask a blessing of his father. Rowland Hill blandly assures children in his *Instructions* that they must respect their parents because 'it was their parents that brought them into life'. This was a poor argument, but not one that children would be likely to question.

A last indication of how much parents regulated their children's lives comes from George Beebee. 'My father had a family of 14 children, and his rule for us in our school days was that we be not out of the house after 7 o'clock. Afterwards, until 21 years of age, his children had to be in the house at 9 o'clock, unless he knew beforehand where they were going and why they would be late. And even after that age, if they dwelt at home they clearly understood that the door would be locked at 10 o'clock. ... To this strict rule his children owe much. ... For this rule six preaching sons have blessed their father's memory.'[22]

Perhaps the children comforted themselves with the paradox:

> *Next to the pow'rs which God ordains,*
> *Enjoin submission due;*
> *Obedience to superiors gains*
> *Authority to you.*

RELIGIOUS INFLUENCE BY PARENTS ON CHILDREN

'Where Parental Influence does not convert,' said Cecil, 'it hampers. It hangs on the wheels of evil.'[23]

The influence was almost pre-natal. Whitefield's unborn child, he hoped, would soon be 'born again'. Mrs Treffrey wrote of her son as an infant: 'The Lord knows that I offered him up before he saw the light.'[24] Charles Wesley, pleading for the godly mother, saw the child only as a soul to be saved.

> *My first concern their souls to rear,*
> *And principled with godly fear*
> *In virtue's paths to lead,*
> *The hunger after Thee to' excite,*
> *And stir them up with all their might*
> *To seek the Living Bread.*[25]

That the influence was loving is certain, but it sometimes appears to be stifling. Henry Longden tells how his mother's deliberate striving for his salvation began when he was seven, and Mrs Bernard took her children to her room for private prayer and wept over them.[26]

The influence could also make of the house 'a heaven upon earth' or a dangerous centre of unregulated 'enthusiasm', whichever way one looks at it. A woman writes of her infant son as 'much blessed. He cries aloud for a clean heart, and attends the ordinances with keenness'.[27]

Many more instances could be quoted of mothers who used very strong moral pressure to gain the children's salvation. 'Before we went to school', says Thomas Jackson of his mother, 'she was accustomed to take us with her into the parlour' where she knelt and pleaded with God 'for the salvation of her children'.[28] More doubtful is the conduct of the mother who 'would sometimes take them by the hand, and with weeping eyes say to them, "My dear child, I cannot be at rest till I see a work of grace begun in your heart".'[29]

Just as Venn recommended the use of a letter to be delivered at the death of a parent to an erring child, so we find in the *Arminian Magazine* of 1778 an intensely spiritual letter from a woman then dead, inserted 'chiefly for the Benefit of her Daughters. God grant they may tread in their Mother's steps!'

A LITTLE CHILD SHALL LEAD THEM

If parents had such great influence on their offspring, the children could also assert influence. Their remarks under religious guidance could also be rather disconcerting to a fond parent. One small boy assured his father 'he had another father in heaven, whom he loved better'.[30] Other children felt that parental influence was not sufficiently godly. One of Janeway's small boys 'would go to his father and mother ... and beg of them to take more care of the souls of his brethren and sisters'.

Some unfortunate children had ungodly parents. Wesley, who saw good in all men, was much deceived in his abominable brother-in-law, Westley Hall. Charles Wesley knew him better, and wrote a hymn proclaiming his soul in hell, but his son's in heaven. Ungodly parents were a problem the Evangelicals encountered early.

When, at the beginning of our period, child converts frequently met opposition from their parents, directions had to be laid down. Wesley was prepared to separate families— and thought it necessary—if parents were 'of the world'. Whitefield took a similar view, and was accused of this responsibility for 'parents condemning their children, and children their parents'. Walker of Truro also approved of separation in aggravated circumstances, and his preliminary questions suggest how difficult it could be. 'If you have warned them of their faults, has it been with modesty and trembling? Have you covered those faults?'[31] He finally had a test case to resolve his doubts, and concluded: 'I think the honour due to parents is not implicit and blind.'[32]

Cases such as that of John Oliver, who was reduced to 'a mere skeleton' by the cruelties of his Methodist-hating father,[33] show to what terrible persecution children could be subject. It is amazing that filial duty should have survived it. On the other hand, it would be profoundly irritating to be reproved for ungodliness (and this term covered many harmless ways, as well as gross sins) by one's own children. And it would be infuriating to listen to Charles Wesley's 'Hymn for the Head of an Unconverted Family' being chanted from the attic:

> *My life of faith and prayer*
> *As madness they condemn,*
> *My ways so strict they cannot bear,*
> *So contrary to them:*
> *My counsels they despise,*
> *When kindly I reprove,*
> *And stop their ears, and shut their eyes,*
> *And trample on my love.*[34]

Later, however, as parental persecution of their children's religion became less common, the problem itself finds less and less mention.

The most exalted concern of the children was saving the souls of their parents. *The Dairyman's Daughter* was assiduous in the art, and Pawson's father, formerly a violent anti-Methodist, sought refuge in the stable through his son's influence, because 'he now had a clear sight of his sinful and lost condition, and was brought into such distress, that, like David, he roared for the very disquietness of his soul'.[35] Anna Shipway, one of Rowland Hill's prodigies, a child saint, was so influential on her parents that her father 'many a night ... went to bed with her before the rest of the family, to hear her talk of her Lord and Saviour Jesus Christ'. Adam Clarke, when his parents declined to lead family worship, did so himself at the age of ten.

By the time the *Evangelical Magazine* was publishing such 'Anecdotes' as 'Conversion of a Father by means of his Child', 'The Swearer Reproved by an Infant', the influence of children on parents—ungodly ones especially—had become almost a matter of course.

Naturally, children did not save only their parents. There were others in need.

Some children dispensed godly advice to their brothers and sisters. 'Do not puff yourself up with pride,' said the infant John Woolley to his sister. 'When you receive your wages, which is not much, lay it out in plain necessaries. And if you are inclined to be merry, do not sing songs; that is the devil's diversion; there are many lies and ill things in those idle songs: Do you sing psalms and hymns.'[36] Sarah Henley required more of her little brother and sister; 'She would ... tell them of their lost condition by nature, weep over them and pray with them, that they might be converted and saved from their sinful state.'[37] Adam Clarke converted both his sisters, and little Katherine Mason, dying at thirteen, read to a boy relative the hymn:

> *Stop, poor sinner, stop and think,*
> *Before you farther go:*
> *Will you sport upon the brink*
> *Of everlasting woe?*

We are not surprised to learn that her favourite passage in literature was Pilgrim going through the Valley of the Shadow of Death.[38]

VISITING

The Englishman's home may be his castle, but an Evangelical's home was a sanctum for all other Evangelicals. and a very important visiting-place for evangelical Ministers.

Wesley instructed his Itinerants to visit, and saw that

they did it. Grimshaw spent much of his parochial life visiting, deeming it as important as preaching. Nearly all the Evangelicals both practised visiting and proclaimed its importance. As 'worldly' visitors were discouraged and virtually the only visitors would be fellow Evangelicals, children were isolated almost completely from the world. Even schooling was frequently given at home. This isolation had two inevitable results. It meant, first, that as far as their parents could contrive, children felt they belonged to the evangelical family, that they were exclusive and excluding, that the beginning and end of life and all its purpose was contained in the godly atmosphere of their house. It is no wonder that children rarely shed the influence all their lives. Secondly, it meant that when the children did, in the natural order of things, finally meet the world, they were often ill prepared to meet its difficulties.

HOME LIFE OF MINISTERS

Ministers have their own peculiar problems. It is their duty in public to be saints, and if their children do not find them saints in private they may well wonder if the holiness is only sham. The strain of public sanctity makes private sanctity the rarer: nobody can be tempted more than a Minister to relieve his mind in private on his children. The man who is a saint to his own children must be a saint indeed. Nor was it easy to talk about the ways of God in the home. What sounded so well from the pulpit often seemed a little strange from the hearth-rug. The Reverend John Thorpe 'ever found, like many other good people, an unaccountable backwardness to speak in a direct way to his children concerning their eternal state',[39] while a brother Minister thought ordained fathers 'to be pitied. I have found the children of ministers disposed to charge their parents with hypocrisy. Ministers are obliged to hold up the standard of perfect holiness'.[40]

John Wesley had no children, but his brother Charles did, and we know much about his home life. Berridge, a confirmed celibate, unfairly wrote (at least as far as 'Charles' and 'George' were concerned): 'Matrimony has quite maimed poor Charles, and might have spoiled John and George (Whitefield), if a wise Master had not graciously sent them a brace of ferrets.' Charles was always more likely to make a success of marriage. Instead of desiring advice about his marriage, as John always did, he said tartly: 'I mentioned it [his marriage] to the select band, desiring their prayers, and not their advice.' In fact, Charles, of all the Wesley family, was the only one to make a happy marriage. We might expect that his children were brought up in a strict atmosphere and followed their father into the Church. Of eight children born, only three survived infancy. Two of these were boys, Charles and Samuel. Both became professional musicians. Neither seriously followed in his father's religious ways, and one even deserted Methodism to turn Papist, but later changed his mind. Charles Wesley tried not to force his own beliefs on his children, but hoped that, by the happiness of their home life, they would want to find the way to God that he had found.

The remaining child, a girl called Sarah, had been pretty as a small child, but the ravages of smallpox had made her ugly. At this 'her father rejoiced that a strong temptation was thus removed from the girl's path'.[41] He tried to teach her himself, but his impatience proved a stumbling-block. On one occasion, infuriated by her failure to understand, he shouted: 'Sarah, you are as stupid as an ass!' At her 'meek and affectionate look of surprise, he burst into tears, adding, "And as patient".' Yet he could be gentle with her too, and everywhere in his letters we sense the man who longs for his daughter to feel about God as he does, yet fears to put it to the test. So it was that he never demanded of her what he demanded of others of his flock. His chief concern, indeed, was to avoid forcing her will. 'Her father did not press her to meet in Society, lest anything might prejudice her against religion,' says Telford. This was an astonishing forbearance in a man as dedicated as Charles Wesley. Yet in spite of it, or because of it, he muses sadly in his *Journal*: 'Why am I not as useful to my own daughter?'[42]

Some of the leading Evangelicals, such as Berridge, Walker of Truro, and Isaac Milner, were celibates; others, like Wesley, Fletcher, and Rowland Hill, had no children; and several, though they had children, say little or nothing about them. Whitefield records the deaths of his infant children very movingly, but says little else. Howell Harris is an even more striking example. There is no reference whatever to his child in his autobiography, though he had at least one daughter. Perhaps this is less surprising in the light of the two brief mentions of his wife, namely, her marriage and her death. A letter to her suggests their relationship was important chiefly in its religious aspect: 'My dear wife, shall this find thy spirit bowing to the great compassionate Redeemer? Weeping before him, for all thy backslidings from him?' This was written for their eighteenth wedding anniversary. Ironically, the only reference to his daughter is on his tombstone where we read of the child 'who was the constant object of their prayers . . .'.

Some Evangelicals clearly considered (one hopes through humility) their wives and children of comparative unimportance compared to the great tasks they had to do. Yet nearly all of them not only loved children, but dealt easily and happily with them: Fletcher above all, and the blind John Crosse, whom children led everywhere, and Isaac Milner, who, like Charles Wesley, never forced belief and was wary even of talking religion.

Those who had children were faced, as Charles Wesley was, with two opposing dangers: that of sickening the children by too much religion at home, and that of giving the impression that parents did not really care whether or not the children shared their parents' views.

Some deliberately sought the salvation of their children at an early age. Grimshaw writes joyfully: 'Two under my own roof are just now under true conviction: one a girl about 18 . . . and a boy about 14 [these were presumably servants]: and I hope my own little girl, between 10 and 11 years old. It is near six months since she first began to show a serious concern for her sinful state.'[43] The sad story of Grimshaw's drunken son seems even more pathetic in the light of this letter. Similarly, a clergyman with ten children, newly converted to the evangelical viewpoint, writes to Isaac Milner that 'a work of grace is begun and advancing in two of my elder sons, in consequence of my domestic ministry ...'.[44]

Two households may be singled out for more detailed examination, those of Henry Venn and Adam Clarke. Both were particularly happy ones, and typical of the best.

Henry Venn's maid, Ruth, announced a visitor: 'A man wants to speak to you about his soul.'[45] It was in this atmosphere that the children lived. Yet it was a very happy atmosphere. Venn was deeply affectionate, devoted to his children, and this spirit of love breathes through all his letters. But his letters are *all* God—especially to the children. A letter to Catherine begins, 'Rising before any one in the family, on this blessed day of Sabbath, I write to my dear Kitty, wishing her not only to refrain from polluting the Lord's day by idle talk ...', and on Eling's birthday she receives a sermon with the reiterated text—'I am the Lord's'; on yet another birthday the girl receives—'not a fine gown; a ring; a Diamond—Another kind of present I am going to make to you, my beloved Powe, in which I know you will rejoice, and I trust, reap profit from it. It is a present for your mind—it is an exposition on the whole state and circumstances of the children of Israel.'[46] Elsewhere she is urged to send notes of all the sermons she hears.

'Whoever sojourns but a day with the members of Christ should perceive, that to love and fear God is their joy.' That was Venn's own claim for his household, and the subsequent careers of his children substantiate it. In their home they 'saw no company but of the Ministers or Children of God ... heard no corrupt communication; no praises, in the warmth of a sensual heart, of beauty, good eating, jollity, or wealth ...', and while in this atmosphere, safe from outer contamination, Henry Venn waited long, as he later told his son, for 'your conviction, by a Divine power, of which you assented to through force of education'.[47]

In the last phrase lies Venn's own theory, that it was impossible to avoid salvation if the religion of the home was right. Certainly it was a happy home, and certainly the children grew to emulate their father's goodness. Perhaps it takes a saint like Henry Venn to succeed with his children in this way.

Adam Clarke was a Methodist, Venn of the Establishment, and Clarke had been one of Wesley's Itinerants while Venn spent his life in two Vicarages, at Huddersfield and Yelling. Their systems for training their children were utterly different, yet both were successful.

Clarke is an attractive personality. Of his twelve children, six died in infancy, but three girls and three boys survived. His evening routine when he was at home explains their love for him. When his work was finished, he would open his study door and shout: 'Come all about me!' From all corners of the house the children hurried to climb on him. Then, with children crawling all over him he would parade round and round the room. After this followed Prayers at their Mother's knee, and then Clarke himself put them all to bed. A 'companion in their play', he invented moral fairy tales for them, and kept supplies of tops, whips, and hoops, in exchange for which he expected some useful thing to be done. The children were not allowed to receive money from visitors and he was careful rarely to praise them directly, but his régime was liberal. So also do his letters contrast with Venn's. They are homely, gentle, and affectionate. They tell of the goodness that was in him, but they do not make demands of the children. Like Charles Wesley, Adam Clarke believed in example more than precept, but like Venn, he was blessed with his children.

Later writers marvelled at the greatness of the evangelical Fathers and concluded that it was the spirit in the home

that had made them great. 'The whole process of education
was conducted with reference to religion,' said William
Beal, and he began to reminisce about his own boyhood.
'What vivid impressions, to this moment, do some of us
retain of our Sabbath evenings, when our pious and judicious
parents, in order to create an early association in our minds
of pleasing thoughts with holy time, granted us that high
privilege, so well known in the dialect of the nursery by the
phrase "sitting up to supper".'[48]

ITINERANTS AND THEIR CHILDREN

Much depended on the Circuit in which they travelled.
The fortunate ones were in cities and managed to live a
settled ministry. The majority travelled wide country
Circuits and to them 'Home' was an almost meaningless
word. As has been suggested in the case of Howell Harris,
many Itinerants were able scarcely to consider their wives
and children. While the father preached on tour, wives and
children made what shift they could to keep alive. Their
sufferings were often as great as those of the head of the
family. While he was an Itinerant, Adam Clarke records how
he bought his children bread when they landed to meet him
from a ship, and how the infant boys, ravenous with hunger,
'buried their little heads in it'. Thomas Taylor's child once
had to travel on 'a kind of floating hell' where the fare was
'a little very bad bread, and some stinking water'.[49]

Wesley rightly discouraged his Itinerants from marriage
and, when they did marry, arranged for the education of
their children (usually at Kingswood), and for some small
allowance for their wives. Nothing, however, could make
their lives pleasant for them. The scant references of the
Itinerants themselves, and of their biographers, make
conclusions about their futures a mystery. It would not be
surprising if these religious orphans hated the very thought
of religion—but one cannot argue from silence.

SUNDAY AT HOME

'The strict observance of Sunday was a marked character-istic of evangelical religion.'[50] It is difficult to determine how children reacted to it. Some certainly reacted violently, such as T. W. Hill, who later wrote: 'When the prayer of Sunday night was concluded, my feelings I was used to compare with those of Christian when his burden was miraculously unstrapped and fell from his back.'[51] But we have not only Mrs Trimmer's assurance that Sunday was not a 'day of gloom and severity', but that it held 'all the pleasures of domestic happiness and quiet enjoyment' (as a parent she was biased):[52] we have also the tacit approval of hundreds of children who lived under a Sabbath 'strictly sanctified', as Adam Clarke phrased it, and in their turn observed it.

In most cases virtually nothing was allowed except reading godly books (and this was usually interpreted as meaning the Bible alone). The day, however, was punctuated by services, and to a child almost imprisoned at home, this would be a welcome diversion. Further, if the children were not allowed to play, this was less a restriction in homes where play at any time was regarded dubiously, and at least there was no compulsion to work. No doubt, as children will, they made the best of it: indeed, they must have enjoyed it, or it would never have been perpetuated. Not for the first time, the impression left is that the children's reactions largely depended on the nature of the parents. Rules of themselves rarely make for misery: it is the application of them that matters.

SCHOOL

THE STATE OF EIGHTEENTH-CENTURY SCHOOLS

It is easy to paint the condition of eighteenth-century schools in too dark colours, but even easier to contradict this view by a few carefully chosen quotations. Against descriptions of the Public Schools as 'nurseries of all manner of wicked-ness' (Wesley), 'the nurseries of all vice and immorality'

(Fielding), and 'a system of premature debauchery' which could 'only prevent men from being corrupted by the world by corrupting them before their entry into the world' (Sidney Smith) must be balanced Cowper's spiritual help from Dr Nicoll's Confirmation Classes, and Wesley's love of Charterhouse.

In general, the state of Public Schools in the eighteenth century seems bad, and religious instruction at a minimum. The Evangelicals distrusted them deeply. Henry Venn refused to have his son educated at Westminster, and Isaac Milner wrote violently against them. The root objection to them was that they were irreligious. If even Wesley 'entered Charterhouse a saint and left it a sinner',[53] what hope had others?

> *What but a miracle of grace*
> *Could keep my soul within*
> *The mouth of hell, the murderer's ways,*
> *The public schools of sin;*
> *Where troops of young corrupters tried*
> *In wickedness to' excel,*
> *Lewdness their vile delight and pride*
> *Their boasted principle?*[54]

If Public Schools were bad, Grammar Schools seem, with some exceptions, to have been little better. Whitefield found they had 'a natural tendency to debauch the mind, to raise ill passions, and to stuff the memory with things as contrary to the Gospel of Jesus Christ as light to darkness, as heaven to hell'.[55] The Dissenting Academies were probably better, and a good tutor might be best of all, though the Tutorial System in general was unpopular; few tutors were like John Fletcher or Cornelius Winter. There was great variation also in the Private Schools of the country—those run by Dames, by the Squire or Parson. They varied from the standard implied by the much-quoted advertisement in the *Morning Post* of 1788, which I strongly suspect of being a joke ('grate ceare takin of theyre morels and spelin . . .'), to that of the school in which Christopher Hopper taught.

THE NEED FOR BETTER SCHOOLS

The appalling state of the schools was obvious to most thinking men. But it was not merely that the existing schools were bad. A vast proportion of the population received no schooling at all.

Perhaps the first of the Evangelicals to see this and to do something about it was Wesley. His approach, of course, was practical, but he also knew the longing for knowledge that thousands of untutored children possessed. So great was young James Lackington's thirst that he paid $1\frac{1}{2}$d. an hour for being taught to spell, when his wages were $1\frac{1}{2}$d. a week, and he records, 'We allowed ourselves but about three hours sleep in twenty-four';[56] all other time not spent in working was used in learning to read.

The middle classes were expanding rapidly during this period and their new wealth enabled them to spend more on the education of the children. New schools had to be found. At the same time, the social conscience of the people began to demand schools for those who could not afford it. The Charity Schools, largely because they were too close to a church which itself was inactive, were dwindling into decay, and yet the need for which these schools had been founded was greater than ever.

It was out of this need that the Evangelicals launched their attack on illiteracy and ungodliness, determined always to make education subservient to the ends of religion as they knew it.

In general, their influence was exerted through their own educational foundations, but evangelical influence in existing schools is by no means negligible. Early in our period Pentycross, as a boy at Christ's Hospital, had such an ascendancy that he produced plays with younger boys. He worried about this use of their time, and assembled them instead 'for serious instruction and prayer'.[57] Though he gave up this practice before he left school, he always considered it his first step in the religious life.

Rowland Hill, while at Eton, was converted by his elder brother Richard, a convinced Evangelical even in his youth. 'My Dear Brothers,' wrote Richard, 'Though I direct this to Rowley, yet it is equally intended for one as well as the other of you, and I hope it will find you both pressing forward towards the prize of high calling of Christ Jesus that is set before you. Letters to inquire after our poor perishing bodies are common enough, but, alas! how few are wrote with a single view of promoting the salvation of our precious immortal souls. . . .' Rowland formed a religious society there, apparently without serious protest from anyone in authority.

Such cases, however, are not common. So absolute in its demand was Evangelicalism that most Evangelicals would rather found schools than content themselves with seeking to influence those already established. Practical difficulties, however, made such foundations rare.

CHARITY SCHOOLS

There is a danger of confusion in using this term. The phrase 'Charity Schools' usually refers to those which began in 1698 under the auspices of the S.P.C.K., and which by the end of the eighteenth century were over two thousand in number but were of very doubtful worth. Instead of being like their ideal, which Blake portrays in his *Songs of Innocence*, they became a bone of contention between Church parties, and centres for fostering 'humility' and 'due reverence for superiors'.

Nevertheless, early in our period several Evangelicals were deep in the S.P.C.K. movement. Whitefield was a corresponding member, and Conyers was also involved. Howell Harris had anticipated Wesley's work by spreading Welsh Charity Schools with Mr Griffith Jones, and William Seward had revived the Charity Schools in London. Charles Wesley had also made his contribution in the 'Hymn for Charity Children':

The meanest worm that creeps on earth
Is not below Thy care;
And we, although of humble birth,
Thy Godlike bounty share.[58]

Evangelicals later founded their own Charity Schools. In practice they differed from the earlier type by the looseness of their attachment to the Church, and a corresponding freedom from set forms in their religious instruction. For set forms they substituted the 'heart-religion' which was the mark of the Evangelical everywhere. Eyre, a Curate of Cadogan's, founded several such schools, as did the Methodists of Lincoln's Inn Fields.

Towards the close of the century charitable schools of every description were started by Evangelicals. It is at this period that evangelical influence began to find itself more at one with the work of the larger Church body. Hereafter, we find the social aims of both parties the same. The revived main Church was as keen as the Evangelicals to educate the poor in a manner fitting their condition.

Attached to Rowland Hill's Surrey Chapel were a school of industry for twenty-four poor girls, and alms-houses for twenty-four poor women. The only way to make serious progress in education seemed to be to prove that it could be done economically. Hence, having proved that charity would redound to the advantage of the giver, all parties began to build schools of industry. It is clear, it should be said in defence of the founders of such schools, that their desire was solely to help the poor, and that they were prepared to give all they could without any desire for repayment on this earth, but it is equally clear that they would receive no help from those less altruistic in their motives than the founders were, unless a sound financial basis for the work could be proved.

In fact the schools were a failure, but there were a number of reasons for this, and a consideration would be out of place here.

More famous than the school of his brother was Sir Richard

Hill's 'Industry Hall'. The instruction given was to enable the pupils 'to procure a livelihood, and fit them to be good and useful servants'. The evangelical note is heard in the promise to give 'all possible attention . . . to sound religious teaching, as the only safe basis of instruction'. A close examination of the timetable, however, suggests that most of the time was devoted to the manufacturing of wool. It is ironical to read a contemporary compliment that Hill 'had anticipated the spirit at least of some of the best plans for the instruction of the lower classes, propounded in this age of education'.[59]

Children with special needs were also remembered. Among Woodd's foundations was a school of industry for orphans, while Wesley, as early as 1742, had founded an Orphan House in Newcastle. Both the name and deeds prove its function, but in fact it was never used as a school until long after Wesley's death.

Hannah More was an excellent practising teacher, a strong Evangelical and a woman of considerable common sense. Her famous Mendip Scheme—it included a series of Day Working Schools—was as well conceived and ordered as such a system could be. Yet it is with a shock that we read her own account of her aims. 'My plan for instructing the poor is very limited and strict. They learn of week-days such coarse works as may fit them for servants. I allow of no writing. My object has not been to teach dogmas and opinions, but to form the lower class to habits of industry and virtue. I know of no way of teaching morals but by infusing principles of Christianity, nor of teaching Christianity without a thorough knowledge of Scripture. . . . To make good members of society (and this can only be done by making good Christians) has been my aim.'[60] This passage was written defensively, but it must be accepted as faithful, and it reads strangely beside Wesley's aims.

EVANGELICAL FOUNDATION OF DAY SCHOOLS

These schools cannot strictly be called Charity Schools, for nominally they charged fees, but in practice (especially at

Wesley's Foundery) fees were rarely taken, and in many cases clothing was provided as well.

We will begin with the Foundery, since it was more directly under Wesley's supervision than his schools at Oxford, Georgia, and Kingswood. There were two masters and about sixty children, most of whom were taught and clothed for nothing. All the children (the youngest was six years old) had to attend the Foundery Preaching, which was at 5 a.m. The School hours were from 6 a.m. to 12 noon, and from 1 p.m. to 5 p.m. Some of the rules were that there were to be no holidays, that no speaking in school was allowed except to the masters, and that absence on two days of one week meant automatic expulsion.[61]

It sounds a rigorous life. A compensation, however, must have been found by all the pupils when in 1744 Silas Told became head-master of the school. Silas Told had led an extraordinary life before he arrived at the Foundery (he went there because 'Mr Wesley positively insisted upon it'), and it was while he was there that he felt he should visit condemned malefactors at Newgate and accompany them to Tyburn tree. Both his reminiscences as an ex-sailor and his gruesome tales from Tyburn must have sweetened the pill of instruction.

The Foundery appears to have been discontinued in 1772, but by 1808 it was again in use as a school of industry for girls. This is typical of the tendency of the times.

Considerably less is known about Old Kingswood, and confusion has arisen over apparent discrepancies in Wesley's own account. The explanation appears to be that Wesley had four schools operating in the same building: a day-school for Colliers' sons, and a day-school for Colliers' daughters, a boarding-school for orphan girls, and a school for adults.

That the children at Bristol, like the children at the Foundery, were expected to join in the religion of their community, is made certain by a letter of John Cennick's of September, 1739: 'I was preaching at the school on the Forgiveness of Sins. . . . Large flashes of Lightning, and loud claps of Thunder, mixt with the screams of frightened Parents, and the Exclamations of nine distressed Souls! . . . many roaring up and down, crying, 'The Devil will have me!' . . . Ten thousand Devils are about me!" '

A number of Wesley's Itinerants were able to educate their children at his day-schools, but no evidence tells us how they were boarded. Other Evangelicals also took the opportunity. Jane Grimshaw, a daughter of Grimshaw of Haworth, died at Kingswood in 1750, when she was thirteen years old. This is the more strange since Grimshaw himself kept a large school. But Wesley's ascendancy over his contemporaries was considerable, and his reputation as a teacher was great.

Other Evangelicals founded day-schools. Henry Venn founded one in 1778 'out of love to the children of my parish'. He engaged a schoolmaster to teach them and was so happy at the results that he wrote: 'Had I my time to begin again, I would give myself more to this work.'[62] So also did Conyers found a school and Thomas Adam make of a Parish Clerk, a Schoolmaster to provide a cheap education for local children. The children were not required to attend services at dawn, but all attended the morning prayers at church on Wednesdays, and some attended a Thursday lecture.

We know little about the schools of the Evangelicals, Wesley's apart, for they were not theorists in the sense that Wesley was, nor were their educational ambitions his. They simply saw a need for a school in their own locality, formed one, and did their best to see that it was a God-centred school. That was enough for them.

But it was not nearly enough for Wesley.

THE FOUNDATION OF KINGSWOOD SCHOOL

Wesley had extravagant hopes of Kingswood. It was to be a school 'which would not disgrace the apostolic age'. 'Behold, Paradise opened in the wild,' he exclaimed, on seeing it complete. It was to be the proof of all his theories, and the fulfilment of all his academic hopes for the future. It was planned with great care. His indictment of contemporary schools was that they were often in large towns, with the inevitable distractions of such surroundings, that the pupils were not selected carefully, that the Masters were frequently incompetent and irreligious, and that the schools were defective in instruction. Wesley notes with astonishment that 'there are some schools of note wherein no Hebrew at all is taught'. Not only was Kingswood to be a School but a University. The Expulsion of the Methodist Students from Oxford in 1768 made this a necessity.

Accordingly, Wesley built Kingswood well outside Bristol, and he selected the pupils with great care, 'such as had some thoughts of God, and some desire of saving their souls: and such whose parents desired they should not be almost, but altogether, Christians'. Parents had to agree that the children must obey all the rules and that they would not leave the school, even for a day, until their schooling was over.

To answer his third argument against contemporary schools, that the masters were incompetent and irreligious, Wesley went to immense trouble to find suitable men. His success in this—or lack of it—will be considered later.

The defects of instruction were answered more easily. Wesley's syllabus for his pupils is an astonishing one. The subjects taught were reading, writing, arithmetic, English, French, Latin, Greek, Hebrew, history, geography, chronology, rhetoric, logic, ethics, geometry, algebra, physics, and music. Though in the First Class (the youngest were six years old) the children 'begin learning to write', a year later they were expected to read *Praelectiones Pueriles*, translate them into English, and the *Instructions for Children* into Latin. All the texts used were moral and religious, written or edited by Wesley himself, 'that nothing immodest or profane' might corrupt the pupils. Every effort was made to

> *Unite the pair so long disjoin'd,*
> *Knowledge and vital piety*—[63]

and the pupils 'worked always with an eye to eternity'.[64]

Kingswood was not primarily intended for the sons of Itinerants, but Wesley's practical eye soon saw what an advantage the inclusion of such boys would have on the itinerant system. They were therefore allowed to become boarders free. Hereafter the problem of the families of Itinerants was made much easier. In 1788 Kingswood changed its function and was used largely for Ministers' sons. Today it still serves both purposes.

The rules of Kingswood were responsible for most of the attacks made on Wesley's whole scheme. The children rose at 4 a.m. and spent the next hour at devotions. At 5 a.m. Public Worship was held. School hours were from 7 a.m. to 12 noon, and from 1 p.m. to 5 p.m. Private prayers were at 5 p.m., the next hour employed in walking or working, and at 7 p.m. a Public Service was held again. The children went to bed at 8 p.m. All intervals in this scheme were filled by work, for no play was allowed. Nor was it ever possible for a boy to be out of sight of a master. Continual surveillance was strictly imposed, and to that end a lamp burned in the only dormitory all night.

These latter two rules were unusual and were criticized. Wesley, however, was sure of their rightness, and insisted: 'Particularly, that the children should never play: and that a master should always be present with them.'

Whatever their appropriateness, the reasons for these two rules are clear enough. It was not merely that 'he that plays when he is a boy, will play when he is a man. If not, why should he learn now what he must unlearn by and by?' It was also that Wesley desired to eliminate from Kingswood all that could interfere with religious development, and the wild horseplay that often occupied leisure at the Public Schools was not consistent with Christian conduct. The surveillance rule was even more closely associated with Wesley's theory. If Baptismal innocence was to remain, then the devil must not be permitted to have even one second in which to work.

WHAT WENT WRONG?

Critics of Wesley's theory of education were numerous in his own day, but Southey, a little later, was probably the most outspoken. 'No man was ever more thoroughly ignorant of the nature of children', he asserts, assures his readers that Wesley's ideas 'must also have done great evil', and considers the practice at Kingswood 'too rigorous and too monastic for the age and country'. As for the rule of no holidays: 'No rule could better forward the purpose of those who desire to enslave mankind.'

More recent critics are scarcely less scathing. One says Wesley's system 'was admirably calculated to make them either lunatics or hypocrites'.[65] Another accuses him of basing his system 'on what the child mind ought to be like',[66] rather than on what he thought it was like (thereby begging the question). Another says, 'Wesley never considered the child as a child, but rather as a unit for salvation, bred in sin, apt to evil, and altogether as "a brand plucked from the burning" ';[67] and the gentlest of all critics of Wesley reluctantly admits that 'John Wesley and the first Methodists failed to understand the outlook of the child'.[68]

As far as the practice of the early years at Kingswood was concerned, this criticism is fully justified, but it does not really disprove Wesley's theory. Though the rules of entry enabled some to come at six years of age and some as late as sixteen (to become members of the 'University of Kingswood') Wesley never had children young enough to be free from worldly contamination before they arrived. His first thesis is not therefore disproved—nor ever likely to be.

Wesley's whole theory, as suggested in Chapter 2, was foredoomed to failure because of his assumption that all children were as he had been—and unless he could have moulded them to his own pattern almost from birth it was bound to be too late when they reached school age. But however impracticable it was in theory, the critics fail to note how great a success it became for the few years before Wesley's death.

The historians of Kingswood School accuse him of failure in 'forgetting that human nature existed in boys as well as in men'.[69] But Wesley was noted for refusing to accept it in men; the demands he made of his helpers were super-normal. It was not Wesley that failed, but human nature.

One must admit that his theory, if not disproved, was hopelessly impracticable. This, however, was not the only reason for Kingswood's early failure to fulfil all Wesley's hopes of it.

A continual problem was that of suitable staff. Wesley made no demands of others that he did not make of himself, but he would be very fortunate to find suitable men 'who were truly devoted to God, who sought nothing on earth, neither pleasure, nor ease, nor profit, nor the praise of men', who were also up to Wesley's exacting standards in academic ability, and who were prepared to spend their lives in continual supervision of boys. Wesley writes despairingly of searching the three kingdoms, and the early years of Kingswood were spent in removing Masters who failed to live up to Wesley's ideal, and in replacing them with others who were often less suitable. Not until 1766 did Wesley find his ideal Master in Joseph Benson, and even Benson only stayed three years. An added difficulty was that the Masters were commonly preachers, not teachers, and not a few left to answer their real vocation. Finally Wesley was obliged to ask prospective Masters if they intended to stay.

Nor was Wesley more fortunate in his female staff. Sarah Ryan had three husbands living when she became Housekeeper at Kingswood, and, notwithstanding her conversion, she seems a highly unsuitable person in a boys' boarding-school. Another Housekeeper, Mary Davey, seemed more concerned with the state of her soul than with the welfare of the boys. When she does mention them, it is to assure Wesley that 'the spirit of this family is a resemblance of the household above. As far as I can discern, they are given up to God, and pursue but the one great end.'[70] Other female servants of the school also write—but always about the state of their own souls.

Wesley became disillusioned. Everything had gone wrong. Suitable Masters could rarely be found, in spite of all his precautions there was corruption among the boys, and the rules were continually being broken. 'The necessity of such an asylum induced him to persevere in it,' says Southey, yet the ominous question 'Shall we drop the School at Kingswood?' was asked at the Conference of 1758. Wesley struggled on. 'I will kill or cure: I will have one or the other —a Christian school, or none at all.' But even when he appeared to have a Christian school something seemed amiss. 'They are all in health: They behave well: They learn well: but alas! . . . there is no life in them.' Still Wesley would not relax his rules.

In 1782 Adam Clarke went to Kingswood for thirty-one days, which he considered thirty-one days too long. His account of it shows the shocking state it was in. Not only were the rules ignored, the Headmaster and his wife utterly incompetent, and the School in a state of chaos, but 'they mocked at religion, and trampled under foot all the laws. The little children of the preachers suffered great indignities: and, it is to be feared, their treatment there gave many of them a rooted enmity against religion for life.'[71] Probably because of the reports of Adam Clarke, Wesley had another purge of Kingswood, and this was to be the last.

From the point of view of religious education, the most signal failures were those of the famous Revivals of 1768, 1770, and 1773. Wesley was concerned in the latter two and a remote admirer of the first, so he should accept some responsibility for them. Though he persisted in his ideas of religious education, writing his famous *A Thought on the Manner of Educating Children* in 1783, one would have thought that the experiences of the Revivals would have made him doubtful of the religious atmosphere that was the very essence of his School.

If—and Wesley had ample proof of it—most of the boys at Kingswood had long lost their baptismal purity, then conversion was the end that must be aimed at. All Evangelicals believed that conversion should be as early as possible, and Wesley was therefore delighted when one of the Masters, Hindmarsh, wrote in April 1768[72] to tell him of the scenes that had been witnessed of boys screaming in remorse and crying with joy at their salvation. Hindmarsh actually wrote his letter to a background of howls and screams.

The second Revival in 1770[73] was even more remarkable. Wesley had preached to the School on a Sunday and noticed an unusual religious seriousness among the boys. Three days later Hindmarsh took them to see the corpse of a neighbour who had died three days before, and followed it up by an evening meeting 'suited to the occasion', and the singing of the hymn,

> *And am I born to die,*
> *To lay this body down?*

Cries for forgiveness soon drowned all else, and, to quote Southey, 'the scene which ensued was worthy of Bedlam'. Fasting, praying, screaming for forgiveness, crying with joy continued for several days until all the boys and several of the maids were 'converted'. Finally, complete exhaustion ended this Revival. Less than a year later Wesley wrote: 'What is become of the wonderful work of grace which God wrought in them last September? It is gone! It is lost! It is vanished away!'[74] A similar comment follows the last Revival. 'I found there had been a fresh revival of the work of God. . . . But it was soon at an end, which I impute chiefly to their total neglect of private prayer.'[75]

If Wesley did not deliberately work up a hysterical atmosphere, as Hindmarsh and Rankin clearly did, he certainly approved what was done, and on other occasions we find him persuading the children towards conversion. Hindmarsh's morbid use of the death of a neighbour to rouse the emotions of his charges is only an extension of the common-place evangelical love of death-beds: it can be paralleled many times. When a child at Kingswood died of the smallpox, Wesley records his funeral and adds: 'And God thereby touched many of their hearts in a manner they never knew before.'[76] Death, most Evangelicals considered, was the best way of persuading children to God. The incident which led to the pathetic entry, 'Willie Darney, a preacher's boy . . . Physic 2s., To Doctor's Bill £1. 3s. 9d., to Coffin, Shroud, etc., 19s.,'[77] was wasted if it did not bring some of the dead child's fellows to fear and repentance. Yet the Revivals had been a failure, and Wesley admitted it. Not only had they been a failure in so far as the lives had not been materially altered, but they had also been used by his enemies to pour scorn on any form of conversion. The cleverest attack took the form of a letter (clearly fraudulent, since the alleged 'Old Boy' did not know the name of his school) printed in Lackington's *Memoirs*. 'It is true, indeed, the work was sometimes attended with power among the children at King's School. Conversions were frequent: but never durable. I myself was converted some 10 or a dozen times. . . . A general conversion among the boys was once effected . . . one poor boy only excepted, who unfortunately resisted the influence of the Holy Spirit; for which he was severely flogged, which did not fail of the desired effect, and impressed proper notions of religion on his mind.'

In theory it was wrong and in practice it was worse.

SUCCESS

Yet Kingswood School before Wesley died was a success—a success even by Wesley's standards. In July 1786 he visited the School and found it 'now one of the pleasantest spots in England. I found all things just according to my desire: the Rules being well observed, and the whole behaviour of the children showing that they were now managed with the wisdom that cometh from above.'[78] Since Wesley was not a man to have been deceived in the matter of rules, and since his stay was not a brief one, we can only assume that in spite of all the set-backs of years Kingswood was now working precisely as its founder intended. Three years later Wesley makes his last important entry about it in his *Journal*, and again it is on a note of thanksgiving that he writes. 'Everything is now just as I wish . . . several [of the children] are much awakened, and a few rejoicing in the favour of God.'[79] The critics who point the finger of scorn at Kingswood ought to explain why, for the last years of Wesley's life, it was not a failure, but a 'sweet success' to a man who had spent thirty-eight years looking for faults in his own system, and at last could find none.

The subsequent history of Kingswood School up to 1800 was one of fluctuating opinion—sometimes Wesley's own theories being enforced, sometimes a more liberal approach being recommended. It is safe to say that by 1800 Wesley's experiment had been virtually abandoned, so proof of its efficacy as a lasting system is lacking. Nevertheless, if the theory in practice is not proven, neither is it disproven, nor is it likely ever to be tried again.

WHITEFIELD'S ORPHAN HOUSE IN AMERICA

Since Kingswood and the Orphan House were in different continents and an estrangement allowed the two founders to meet only rarely, any parallels between the two systems must show a pattern of evangelical education outside the personalities of the two men. Indeed, Wesley and Whitefield were temperamentally very different. Wesley was a master logician, Whitefield rash and impetuous; Wesley was a brilliant strategist, Whitefield only a competent tactician, who left larger issues to look after themselves; Wesley kept a very close eye on all his projects, Whitefield left his Orphan House untended for months, sometimes for years.

Yet the parallels are still striking. The very purpose of the Orphan House reads like that of Kingswood, except that the Orphan House was mixed, and intended for children who would have to earn their living without any help.

'Whoever among them appears to be sanctified, and have a good natural capacity, I intend, under God, for the Ministry. . . . Girls . . . taught such things as may make them serviceable. . . . Though the children are taught to labour for the meat that perisheth, yet they are continually reminded to seek first the kingdom of God and his right, and then to depend upon God's blessing on their honest endeavours for having food and raiment added unto them.'[80]

So also, allowing for the different purpose of the School, does the daily routine of the Orphan House read like Kingswood's. They rose at 5 a.m., spent time in private prayer, and had Public Worship at 6. A shorter service followed at 7, and breakfast followed it. Intervals were filled by hymn-singing. From 8 to 10 the children worked at carding or spinning or shoe-making, and from 10 to noon they had school lessons, after which they dined. Until 2 p.m. 'everyone was employed in something useful, but no time was allowed for idleness or play which are Satan's darling hours to tempt children to all manner of wickedness, as lying, cursing, swearing, or uncleanness'.[81] The rest of the day was divided into service, work, and lessons. Since the children went to bed at 9 they had been up exactly as long as the boys at Kingswood.

Just as Kingswood had its troubles, so did the Orphan House, and Whitefield was as appalled as Wesley at the acts of some of his charges. So also did Whitefield deliberately seek the salvation of the children. 'As my design in building the Orphan House was to build up souls for God, I endeavour to preach most of all to children's hearts. . . . The power of God has been frequently visited among them. Many of the girls seem to be tender hearted. Several of the boys have been under strong convictions.'[82]

The most curious parallel, however, is that when Revivals began at the Orphan House it was during the absence of the founder. As Wesley had, Whitefield received the information by letter that children were 'allowed to spend two or three hours every day in reading, praying, and singing hymns together'.[83] The scenes of cries and tears and screams are just as they were at Kingswood.

The pattern, then, of evangelical education in a boarding-school is clear. The centre of all the work is religion: the supreme aim is the salvation of the souls of the children, and the immediate aim is an early conversion.

GIRLS' SCHOOLS

Wesley theorized a good deal about schools for girls. Large boarding-schools taught 'pride, vanity, affection, intrigue, artifice', he thought, and advised: 'If you cannot breed them up yourself, send them to some mistress that truly fears God.' There were, he believed, several mistresses who truly feared God, and he frequently commends them: Miss Owen, Miss Bishop, Mary Bosanquet, and the Misses Yeomans. He corresponded regularly with the first three. Wesley also wrote *A Female Course of Study, only intended for those who have a good understanding and much leisure*, and published rules for a girls' school which were merely a repetition of the Kingswood rules.

Mary Bosanquet's school was for the poorest of all children, most of them orphans who, when admitted, 'were naked, full of vermin, and some of them were afflicted with disagreeable distempers'.[84] Notwithstanding this, Mary Bosanquet attempted to give these children a Christian education not unlike Wesley's at Kingswood, except that two short periods were allowed for 'play, or instruction, or recreation' (this presumably depended on the age of the children). There were two periods for worship: the eldest girls 'arose between 4 and 5: the younger not much later'. Only two teachers looked after the children, Miss Bosanquet and Sarah Ryan (formerly Wesley's housekeeper at Kingswood). No evidence points to any attempts at conversion. All accounts agree that Mary Bosanquet's instruction was as much by example as by precept.

Teachers such as Mary Bosanquet were rare, and Wesley was not the only critic of girls' boarding-schools. The Rev.

Mr Kinsman wrote to the *Evangelical Magazine* in 1794 complaining about his daughter's school, anxious that there should be less dancing, and more prayer. All critics agreed—non-evangelicals also—that girls' boarding-schools tended to encourage snobbery.

Hannah More raised her requirements according to the nature of her pupils. She taught many types. Her own boarding-school in Bristol was emphatically for 'young ladies' and she had visiting masters for highly un-evangelical pursuits such as dancing and music. She was probably, however, a very good teacher, and believed in the largely unconsidered matter of making her teaching interesting. In her *Strictures on the Modern System of Female Education* she insists that dull learning by rote be replaced by 'animated conversation and lively discussion'. Like Christ, a teacher should instruct by 'interesting parables'; should seize on 'surrounding objects and local circumstances'. The teacher should 'call on all creation to her aid' and so make religion enjoyable, 'and her ways appear, what they really are, the ways of pleasantness'.

All this sounds modern and enlightened, and there is evidence that it was so. Unfortunately for her reputation as a teacher, Hannah More found herself forced to defend her educational schemes against critics who considered the education of the poor politically dangerous. If people like Hannah More had their way, they argued, there would be no more servants, no more underprivileged poor to work for the wealthy.

It is in reacting against this charge that Hannah More often sounds harsh and unimaginative. The same woman who to her pupils was 'gay, friendly, indulgent, sometimes too indulgent',[85] who had cats called 'Non-resistance' and 'Passive obedience', deliberately taught poor girls only what would fit them for servants, urged the workers to be content with their bad conditions, and 'rejoiced that' the pauper children of her schools 'knew tolerably well the first twenty chapters of Genesis'.[86] Enlightened as she was, Hannah

More was yet a child of her age; she must be judged as such.

Numerically speaking, girls' schools under evangelical influence were small, partly because their very function was suspect by the Evangelicals. Those that did exist vary considerably in quality, from the converted Charity School in York which, falling on evil days, was refounded in 1785 and became a flourishing Spinning School under evangelical influence, to the unhappy Cowan Bridge School under Carus Wilson, which achieved notoriety as 'Lowood Institution' in *Jane Eyre*.

SUNDAY-SCHOOLS

The most important educational development of the eighteenth century is the foundation of the Sunday-school, and the education was not, like Kingswood, for a special class—sons of Itinerants and middle-class fee payers—but for those in greatest need, the children of the poor.

Though its best-known founder is Robert Raikes—and justly so, since he organized it—his work was anticipated by earlier Evangelicals. Raikes did not publish his famous article in the *Gloucester Journal* until 1783, but Hannah Ball, a follower of Wesley, gathered children into her High Wycombe Home every Sunday from 1769 to hear them read the Bible and repeat the Catechism. This practice she kept up for many years. Sophia Cooke, a helper of Raikes and another follower of Wesley, anticipated the founder's work in Gloucester itself. She collected children in a church and asked them 'religious questions'.

After Raikes's article of 1783, Wesley approved the scheme and lent all the aid he could. He published a copy of the article in his *Arminian Magazine* and ordered his followers to support the work.

THE PURPOSE OF THE SUNDAY-SCHOOL

The original purpose of the Sunday-school was clearly secular. Raikes began his work by soliciting help for the inhabitants of the Gloucester Bridewell and so realized the ignorance of the prisoners. He taught some of them to read and saw the connexion between 'idleness and crime'. Wesley's characteristic reaction—'Who knows but some of these Schools may become nurseries for Christians?'—proves that the Schools were not so far regarded in this light.

Indeed, there is evidence that some Evangelicals believed that the connexion between ignorance and vice was the primary reason for the Sunday-school. 'An obvious remedy for the evils of popular commotion, is the education of the youth of the lower classes,'[87] says Middleton, clearly assuming this to be its chief function, while the *Evangelical Magazine*, supporting the Schools on social grounds, shows also how important the economics of charity had become: 'If any thing can add to the satisfaction of the reader, it must be the consideration that the teachers . . . give their labours gratis.'[88]

Other Evangelicals seem unsure about its purpose. It is perhaps typical of Hannah More that in one of her tracts (*The Sunday School*) she argues that it will prevent crime: 'Will your property be secured so effectually by the stocks on the green, as by teaching the boys in the school, that for all these things, God will bring them into judgement?' and in the same tract a Mrs Jones founds a Sunday-school for the purpose of learning to read the Bible. There was no inconsistency in her mind. Religion was of practical value: morality is part of it. Similarly, Hanway includes in his book *A Comprehensive View of Sunday School*, a long quotation from 'Defects of Police', the connexion being the purpose of the Sunday-school: yet in the same book he finds the schools 'an admirable expedient for instruction in religious knowledge'.

At the turn of the century there appear to be two distinct views about Sunday-schools. One was the strong evangelical view held by such people as William Hey, who believed that Sunday-schools were to be used solely for religious instruction. He makes the following 'Observations on the Management of Sunday Schools'. (1) That there should be no deviation from the Sabbath. (2) That the whole day should be employed in exercises of religion. (3) That religious instruction is vital. (4) That Sunday-schools are good, but 'should admit of no employment but such as is directly conformable to the appropriate duties of the day'. (5) That learning to write is wrong (the children should only learn to read).[89] The much more widely held theory was that ignorance bred immorality, and the inculcation of 'mere morality', as the earlier Evangelicals called it, was sufficient reason for the work of the Schools. There were, of course, many Evangelicals (probably most) who, like Hannah More, held a midway position between the two theories. But it is possible that those who held the mid-way position, only apparently did so. Since money was vital to the founding of Sunday-schools, Evangelicals may have been forced to use the arguments of Mammon to further the work of God. So deliberately, however, does Hannah More (for instance) harmonize her two reasons for supporting Sunday-school work, that it is probable that the two arguments were considered almost equally potent by many Evangelicals, or even two aspects of the same argument.

SPREAD AND INFLUENCE OF SUNDAY-SCHOOLS

The Sunday-school Movement virtually began in 1780. Not until 1783 was any public mention made of it, but by 1787 250,000 scholars had enrolled. The support, clearly, was tremendous. It warranted support on many grounds: religious, social, political. What began as a doubtful experiment became a national success. Immediately after Raikes's announcement of 1783, it was taken up avidly. Nurtured by the Evangelicals, they also assured its rapid growth.

Few Evangelicals were not actively engaged in Sunday-school work. The Wesleys, Whitefield, Fletcher, Grimshaw, Berridge, Newton, Conyers, Cadogan, Rowland Hill, Venn, Jones, Crosse, were all deeply involved—and what they began the later Evangelicals continued. Wesley's assessment of it as 'one of the noblest institutions which has been seen in Europe for some centuries', assured full Methodist support; the Church of England Evangelicals rallied their supporters, and nearly all dissenting sects supported it, sometimes differing from the others in their refusal to keep it non-sectarian, as Raikes wisely intended.

It was equally popular in the main Church body. Bishop Porteus commended it strongly, but also urged his clergy, possibly as an aside for the benefit of his evangelical brethren, to use 'the utmost caution not to make Sunday a day of rigour, but to maintain it as a day of pleasant rest, by allowing the scholars sufficient time for cheerful conversation and above all, for enjoying the fresh and wholesome air and sunshine in the fields or gardens with their relations and friends'.[90]

In the light of this enormous popularity, it is curious that the Sunday-school had to overcome two considerable obstacles and one violent controversy before its success was assured. One obstacle was social, the other economic.

The social problem was the argument, common at this period, that education for the poor would beget in them a desire to emulate their betters, a refusal to do the work God had appointed them to do, and a subversive attitude which would lead to revolution. This argument was levelled against Sunday-schools, and was only rejected because of the strength of the counter-argument that learning begets a social conscience. Nevertheless, the argument persisted for a considerable time.

The economic problem was even more serious. In 1800 the Sunday-school Movement virtually died out in Gloucester, the city of its foundation, because funds could not be found with which to pay the teachers. It was Wesley's example that saved it. Since 1785 his Sunday-schools had been organized and taught by voluntary helpers. This example others followed and soon after the beginning of the nineteenth century the Sunday-school was almost entirely a voluntary organization.

The Blagdon Controversy, during which the whole future

of Sunday-schools was in the balance, began as a quarrel between the local curate and the schoolmaster, quickly involved Hannah More, and so became an unpleasant *cause célèbre* from 1800 to 1803. Rarely expressed, but deep behind all the personal abuse, was the question whether or not the poor should be educated, and by whom. It was, in fact, the social objection to the Sunday-school Movement in a disguised form. It also inevitably caused trouble between Evangelicals and the main Church body, though it is clear that the curate and schoolmaster were poor examples of each. The only results of the Controversy—if it had any at all— were a brief period of hard feelings between Evangelical and Non-Evangelical, and a fractional check to charitable work. Hanna More's own reputation suffered little damage.

Later minor disagreements about whether or not the Sunday-schools should teach writing on the Sabbath Day had little effect on the total achievement. The Sunday-school Movement entered the nineteenth century immensely strong, supported by all parties. Throughout the last twenty years of the eighteenth century, and influential still for half a century more, the Evangelicals looked upon Sunday-schools as peculiarly their own. Even today the greatest stress on the work is still found among Evangelicals.

THE SUNDAY-SCHOOL IN PRACTICE

Raikes's own system formed the pattern on which most Sunday-schools were based. Fifty boys and fifty girls were in his school. Their day began at 9 a.m., and a neat device of exchanging the children's hats (before lunch, the children's hats were removed and others substituted: they only regained their own during afternoon school) ensured afternoon attendance. Church services were at 12.30 and 3 p.m. and the children went to these. Apart from time for meals, school and worship were continuous until 6 p.m. A system of rewards (using tickets) eventually brought an industrious child a prayer book. Though teaching was secular, school began and ended with prayer. An old lady who had been a pupil at Raikes's school remembered it all with pleasure, but especially remembered Raikes's funeral because they were all given 'a piece of cake as big as a saucer, and a shilling'.[91]

The *Evangelical Magazine*, which gave much publicity to the excellence of Sunday-schools, made its own suggestions about the formation of them. Fifteen or twenty children were enough for one teacher; the schools should be held in the private house of the teacher, in hired rooms, or the church vestry; 'where gratis teachers cannot be found', school masters or mistresses were never to be paid more than two shillings a day; visitors, who were the 'life and soul of Sunday Schools' (presumably of the Lady Bountiful variety), had to give a general inspection, for 'let the visitors remember that religion is the first object of this institution'; the hours of attendance (excluding worship at church) should be from $4\frac{1}{2}$ to 6 hours, for 'religion must not be made gloomy to the children'; punctuality is important, and work should include hearing the Catechism or portions of Scripture and reading and spelling; punishment should be 'withholding those rewards' which virtue earns.[92]

It is clear how much flesh evangelical thought has added to the bare bones of Raikes's scheme. The substance of all the teaching would be evangelical in tone. Instead of the unfortunate example of the curate who 'gave the infant congregation a 12-minute address on the laws of the land and the divine right of kings',[93] the Evangelical would seize the opportunity to remind his hearers that they must die— perhaps soon.

The most eleborate scheme for Sunday-schools is Hanway's *A Comprehensive View of Sunday Schools*. It differs from Raikes's system in a number of ways, and also shows the evangelical emphases.

Classes, he says, should never be mixed, or 'the boys would be the less manly and the girls the less modest'. The work should be 'confined simply to reading' for 'writing is not of a nature proper to be taught them, nor would it be consistent, if it were, for the Sabbath-day'. 'When they have learnt to read, to say their prayers, and the catechism', the Sunday-school can teach them no more.

Work in Sunday-schools, according to Hanway, should begin not with the Bible but with 'moral sentences'. Stories or fables, 'should be founded in truth', though Hanway himself interprets this very loosely. The most important means to the success of a Sunday-school are Prayer and the Zeal of Masters and Mistresses.

Hanway's scheme of work carries children through from complete illiteracy to a fair standard of reading. Preliminary tables, which would interest psychologists deeply, and have a curious and strong evangelical flavour, teach the children to read. Here are the first two words of each table:

I	ba	be
II	all	ake
III	bat	cat
IV	cat	plumb
V	pound	beef
VI	belly	bible
VII	funeral	monument.

Then the Lessons begin, the first on the Duty of a child, later ones on Duty (again), Industry, Humility, etc. After Lesson 5, the Lectures begin, the first on Instruction. After Lecture 3 the Stories begin, the first about Peter Player and Tom Trifler, who waste time. The whole course of Instruction concludes with the Apostles' Creed, the Ten Commandments, and information about the Institution of Baptism and the Duty of Prayer.

Hanway's rejection of the Bible as a beginning found few in agreement. Hannah More found 'the grand object of instruction . . . the Bible itself', and 'the great thing is to get it faithfully explained, in such a way as shall be likely to touch the heart and influence the conduct'.[94] She began with the Parables in St Luke 15, and then 'we dwell for a long time on the first three chapters of Genesis, endeavouring from these to establish them [the children] in the doctrine of the fall of man'. As far as the actual method of instruction is concerned, 'my grand endeavour' is 'to make everything as entertaining as I can',[95] and she did this by 'familiar home-ly language, full of anecdotes of the people round them as well as of the good people that lived in old times, and full of practical piety'.[96]

M. G. Jones says of Hannah More's Sunday-school work: 'To her the problem was a religious, not an economic one.'[97] This, I think, is an over-simplification. The woman who wrote *Village Politics* felt the economic problem deeply. Rather did Hannah More find the economic and religious problems inextricably bound, but thought the religious answer to the problem would settle both.

We find, as we would expect, a number of conversions attributed to the influence of the Sunday-school. Henry Longden, for instance, clearly worked towards it, for he records the foundation of a Sunday-school and after only two meetings we read: 'Two boys were converted at the school today.'[98] Similar cases of conversion occur in Rowland Hill's *Instructions for Children*, where his own Surrey Chapel children lead saintly lives (and deaths) through the influence of their Sunday-school.

Other movements, isolated ones such as Cusson's Meet-ings for Children, or organized ones such as the Schools of Religious Instruction, Sabbath Catechetical Schools, and the much earlier Welsh Circulating Schools, founded in 1737, flourished at this period, all of them near relations of the Sunday-school. Their very existence proves, as part of one great movement, that the Sunday-schools answered an urgent need of the nation. The Evangelicals used the move-ment, in the establishment of which they had played so great a part, to carry on their traditions.

THE CHURCH

THE PRESENCE OF CHILDREN

The relevance here of considering the preaching of the Evangelicals depends on the presence of children. So much was their presence assumed, that a reference to it is rare. For instance, though we know that the Foundery children had to be present at the 5 a.m. preaching, dozens of accounts of those services fail to mention them. It was taken as a matter of course.

Only when their presence had special significance were the children mentioned. One such occasion was the Tabernacle Riot in Plymouth of 1747, when a company of sailors broke into one of Whitefield's services. The brutal assaults on women and children made the whole affair more horrible. Another occasion was when an earth tremor shook the Foundery as Cennick was preaching; the screams of children made the occasion even more frightening.

The very insignificance of children was another reason for mentioning them. Some Itinerants, recounting their travels, tell of their presence only to prove a general lack of interest. Occasionally they are mentioned because of striking appearances, and once because of striking behaviour when Whitefield was preaching in Moorfields. 'I cannot help adding,' he wrote, 'that several little boys and girls were fond of sitting round me on the pulpit, while I preached, and handing to me the people's notes. Though they were often struck with the eggs, dirt, etc., thrown at me, they never once gave way; but, on the contrary, every time I was struck, turned up their little weeping eyes, and seemed to wish they could receive the blows for me.'[99]

But the general impression is that children of evangelical parents were expected to attend worship from a very early age. What was accepted required no notice.

THE IMPORTANCE OF PREACHING

'The Pulpit is a Minister's throne,'[100] said a member of the Eclectic Society, and there are constant references to the importance of preaching in their meetings. Its centrality in worship became an inevitable danger when congregations had to be rebuked for going to hear a powerful preacher rather than going to worship God. This, however, was a compliment to the large number of powerful preachers that the Evangelicals could boast. An even greater compliment is Archbishop Secker's call to the Diocese of Canterbury to adopt 'Gospel preaching', at least in his definition of it.

How did they preach? What was it the children enjoyed or endured? There is considerable variation here. Wesley, as befitted a 'Methodist', made rules for his Itinerants and saw that they were kept. Southey unkindly suggests that the only requisite for an Itinerant was zeal, but this charge seems unwarranted. 'Scream no more, at the peril of your soul,' Wesley ordered a helper who was in danger of becoming a mere 'Gospel-ranter', and he was constantly watching his Itinerants to guard against the taint of enthusiasm.

Wesley prescribed simplicity and brevity as the first two essentials for preachers—an hour was long enough for a service. Newton agreed with him, and also advised careful preparation for preaching.

Other preachers, however, and notoriously Rowland Hill, seemed happier in their preaching without preparation. Hill's method—if it can be called a method—was to speak to his congregation about whatever Christian thoughts came into his head as he entered the pulpit. He drew strange praise from Isaac Milner: 'Mr Hill, Mr Hill, I *felt* today—'tis this slap-dash preaching, say what they will, that does all the good.'[101] Grimshaw ('discretion was no part of his character,' said Southey) and Berridge also observed no rules but their own, and nobody would dare to imitate them. Yet again, personality counts for so much.

Henry Venn, an extempore preacher like nearly all Evangelicals, tried to assist his younger brethren in avoiding the pitfalls of this practice. He said they should write out their sermons for five to seven years, and only after that experience preach extempore, preparing by study, prayer, premeditation and notes.

Public Prayer was considered by Venn as important as preaching, though few would have agreed with him. The manner of praying varied also, but most Evangelicals prayed extempore.

THE POWER OF PREACHING

The sermons which the children heard with their parents were not such as would send them to sleep. On the contrary, the effect the preaching had usually lasted a life-time and influenced the next generation. Wesley, though probably less great a preacher than Whitefield, was still powerful. To read his sermons is not to judge the effect, any more than Whitefield's power can be judged that way. We can only assess his influence from the accounts of his contemporaries. Though he was 'entirely free from some of the extravagances of his followers' and dealt little 'even in impassioned appeals to the terrors of hell',[102] it was Wesley's preaching that started the convulsions that brought early Methodism much notoriety and much abuse. It was principally through Wesley's preaching that the face of England was changed. Perhaps the greatest compliment paid to it was a negative one; some of them said they would not hear him preach for fifty pounds.

Stories of Whitefield's power as a preacher are legion. He was possibly the greatest orator of all time. At twenty-one he 'drove 15 mad';[103] he was acclaimed a genius by Garrick, who said he could make men weep or tremble by his varied pronunciation of the word 'Mesopotamia'; even his enemies recognized his tremendous ability. Perhaps the most remarkable tribute of all is Benjamin Franklin's, since on that occasion a man as determined as Franklin was obliged to change a deep personal prejudice solely through the force of Whitefield's oratorical powers. 'I happened to attend one of his sermons,' he wrote, 'in the course of which I perceived he intended to finish with a collection, and I silently resolved he should get nothing from me. [Franklin disapproved strongly of the purpose of the collection.] I had in my pocket a handful of copper, 3 or 4 silver dollars, and 5 pistoles in gold. As he preached I began to soften, and concluded to give the copper. Another stroke in his oratory determined me to give the silver, and he finished so admirably that I emptied my pockets into the collector's dish.'[104] His oratory could be intensely dramatic, as when he ordered the Archangel Gabriel to pause in his flight while he urged his hearers to let news of their conversion be carried to God, or when he put on his 'condemning cap' to damn lost souls. Yet he could also use language which in anyone else would be ludicrous and blasphemous, as when he asked, 'Has Jesus ever dandled you on his knee?' or when he wrote to Wesley, apparently dying, 'May he kiss your soul away'.

In Grimshaw Whitefield found a kindred spirit. When during the latter's preaching two members of the congregation fell dead, it was Grimshaw who called out: 'Brother Whitefield, you stand among the dead and the dying; an immortal soul has been called into eternity; the destroying angel is passing over the congregation; cry aloud, and spare not!'[105]

If, in his Master's name, Whitefield took great liberties with his congregation, Grimshaw took greater. When the former complimented Grimshaw's parishioners in a sermon, their vicar shouted out: 'Oh, Sir, for God's sake do not flatter them; I fear the greater part of them are going to hell with their eyes open.' His strange style lacked the dignity that Whitefield could employ, but it exceeded the greater preacher in what Grimshaw himself called 'market language'. One biographer happily expresses it as preaching in the same style as that in which Albrecht Dürer painted. Venn explained the same ability more circumspectly: 'And, as in ancient times, before preaching was reduced to such a refinement, and alas! to such a cold and languid exercise . . . his people felt excited in their hearts deep sorrow for sin; and the whole congregation have been often seen in tears.'[106]

Berridge was not less powerful a preacher, as the extraordinary scenes during the Everton 'Revival' attest (fits, convulsions, ravings, screams for mercy, howls of penitence,

and many of them from disbelieving outsiders), while
Newton, another man who used vivid illustrations from
life in making his points, was as able. Rowland Hill also
had an unusual style, and was unable to resist a temptation
to 'clownish antics' in the pulpit. Nearly all Hill's biographers agree on this regrettable tendency, but the only examples they give seem admirably suited to his purposes as a
preacher. When, for instance, during a sermon some people
sheltered from the rain in the church porch, Hill said:
'Many people are greatly to be blamed for making their
religion a cloak, but I do not think those are much better
who make it an umbrella'.[107] Presumably he also indulged in
'market language'.

What was said about Robinson of Leicester, 'He stood
as the messenger of Heaven; and proclaimed, "Thus saith
the Lord" '[108] could be said of all the Evangelicals. The
very nature of the Revival made preaching the centre of
worship. When the early Evangelicals were persecuted and
driven from the churches, they could still preach anywhere.
Holy Communion could not easily be taken outside a church,
but any place was appropriate for preaching: a barn, a
cottage, a garret, a cellar, the village green, a field; all could
be utilized as preaching places, and since little except
preaching was easy in those conditions, and since many of
the Evangelicals had no rights whatever except to preach, it
was to this God-given privilege that they clung. Later,
when preaching-houses were built for them or they were
able to use Dissenting Chapels, it was still to their one
prerogative that they adhered. While Wesley's 'ragged
legion of preaching barbers, cobblers, tinkers, scavengers,
draymen, and chimney-sweepers' (Rowland Hill's spiteful
description of the Itinerants) still preached in the open-air,
their more fortunate brothers in the Establishment used
Lectureships and Proprietary Chapels for their preaching,
but preaching was no less the primary means of grace. 'It
was God's good pleasure through the foolishness of preaching to save them that believe', was a text they often quoted:

their first aim was to save souls, and they knew how it could be done. And this means of grace was always available.

'When my clothes were disgracefully bad I absconded from my own church, and occasionally wandered into a meeting-house,'[109] said William Jay. The Evangelical Revival had spread to every form of Dissent and in all of them it was the preaching that mattered.

SUBSTANCE OF SERMONS

Wesley insisted that his Itinerants should preach both the Gospel and the Law. They should begin with a 'General declaration of the love of God to sinners' and then refer to the Law, 'only intermixing the Gospel here and there'. When 'more persons are convinced of sin' they should preach 'more of the Gospel'. Whitefield was also a preacher of 'Gospel sermons'. 'His 30 or 40,000 sermons were but so many variations on two key-notes. Man is guilty, and may obtain forgiveness; he is immortal, and must ripen here for endless weal or woe hereafter.'[110] Many of them, even in their printed form—a poor substitute—are frightening: 'You are as proud as the devil, and with devils shall you dwell to all eternity. ... All the curses of the Law belong to you. Cursed are you when you go out; cursed are you when you come in; cursed are your thoughts; cursed are your words: cursed are your deeds. Everything you do, say, or think, from morning to night, is only one continued series of sin'.[111] 'The Eternity of Hell Torments,' a fairly common theme among the Evangelicals, Whitefield preached on board ship, a situation of especial fear in those days. 'Hell fire' preaching was by no means new, nor was it a preroga-tive of the Evangelicals, but it was very rarely treated by the Latitudinarian Church and therefore appeared at that period to be peculiarly Evangelical.

Berridge was another remarkable success as a 'Gospel Preacher'. His advice to Gospel Ministers shows how his own sermons were constructed. One should begin by 'laying open the innumerable corruptions of the hearts', then 'declaring every transgression' of the law 'deserving of death', wait until 'your hearers are deeply affected' and then 'wave the Gospel flag. ... Speak it with a full mouth (*ore rotundo*) that his blood can wash away the foulest sin',[112] and so, presumably, conversions would begin.

Cecil admits to using 'hell fire' preaching especially for children. 'I generally have recourse to terrible images. I explain salvation by a house on fire: for I remember, when I was a child, and learned from bad companions to curse and lead a wicked life, I thought I would keep on, if I could but escape hell.'[113] Legh Richmond also habitually preached damnation to children. Most infants of this period felt with Watts that they could only sin haunted by the fears of hell:

> *While all the preachers of thy word,*
> *Warn me to 'scape eternal fire.*

SPECIAL SERVICES FOR CHILDREN

Though children were expected to attend services with their parents, there was a gradual feeling among Evangelicals that they had special needs as children which might be answered best by services for them alone.

Rowland Hill seems to have been early to do this (about 1777), but I have discovered little except that he held them. Wesley held some in 1785 at his City Chapel, but again details are scanty.[114] About the same time Newton used them, 'to reason with them, and explain the Scriptures in their own little way'.[115] In the 1790's Hannah More fitfully held some,[116] and in 1798 the idea was of sufficient importance for the Eclectic Society to debate it.[117] Not until the turn of the century, however, was it recognized practice. In 1804 it was accepted as nothing unusual for Legh Richmond 'to have said Evensong a second time in the evening, as a preliminary to a sermon for the special benefit of the young'.[118]

CONVERSION OF CHILDREN UNDER PREACHING

Examples abound. The end of the Evangelical's task from the pulpit was conversion, and they were as successful with children as with adults.

Under Wesley's preaching it was common. On one occasion he found 'five or six so affected that they could not refrain from crying aloud to God';[119] such an example could be multiplied many times. Under Whitefield it was even commoner; such phrases as 'boys and girls flock in consternation to preachers', 'a boy about 8 ... wept as though his heart would break', 'the Lord is working upon little children', are so common in Whitefield's ministry as almost to be accepted as a matter of course. A fuller example of such scenes reads: 'My little orphans now begin to feel the love of Jesus Christ. ... When we came to church, the power of the Lord came upon all. Most of the children, both boys and girls, cried bitterly. The congregation were drowned in tears. ... It would have charmed your heart to have heard the little ones, in different parts of the house, begging Jesus to take full possession of their hearts. The same power continues today. For near two hours, 4 or 5 girls have been before the Lord weeping most bitterly.'[120]

Whitefield's conversions of children lasted throughout his ministry. So did Berridge's conversions; but at the period of the famous Revivals, conversions of children, as of adults, were wholesale.

That the three men mentioned above were exceptional is true, but conversion of children under other Evangelicals is common enough. They set no limit to an early conversion—indeed, the earlier the better—and their preaching was the same for children as for adults. Conversion was expected.

CHILDREN IN CLASS-MEETINGS

Wesley's organizing genius arranged his followers into Societies. The Society was the local unit, and a preacher would give 'such advice as he deemed better suited to a godly fear'. Only full members of the Church—not merely adherents—were invited to Society Meetings, which were outside hours of Service. Class-Meetings were for full members on week-nights. Each class consisted of twelve or fourteen people. After an abbreviated service, the religious state of mind of each member was ascertained by the Leader, who accordingly offered comfort or correction. The Bands consisted only of 'justified' persons. They were in groups of ten, men or women, single or married. Particular sins were confessed in the examination, and again the Leader gave advice. The highest order was the Select Bands. Members of these had to be 'made perfect in love' before they were eligible.

In addition to these meetings, Wesley instituted three others: Prayer-Meetings, which were held in private houses and were short services with Prayer as the centre instead of a Sermon; Love-Feasts, which were meetings for very little food and drink, but for testimonies; and Watch-Night meetings, held from about 7 p.m. to midnight. These were full services, at which conversions were frequent.

Not only Wesley's followers enjoyed these meetings. Many other Evangelicals adopted similar systems. Rowland Hill, for instance, held Prayer-Meetings; Fletcher formed his own Societies on Wesley's pattern in 1762; and Society Meetings were sufficiently common in the Establishment for their abandonment to be considered with reluctance by the Eclectic Society in 1800.

The religious atmosphere that the Societies offered must have been more intense than most monasteries, and in all but the Select Bands, children—and sometimes very young ones—had a share. It was not common for children to be members of the Societies, but neither was it rare. Thomas Jackson, for instance, attended Class-Meetings when he was under ten, though not really in his own full right until he was sixteen.[121] A certain Mary Smith was in a Class-Meeting for children at eleven, and one for Young Women at fourteen.[122] The presence of children at Class-Meetings is strongly implied elsewhere at Wesley's City Road Chapel,[123] and openly asserted in detail at Kingswood.[124] Indeed, at Kingswood the higher term 'Bands' is employed.

Since 'the greatest part of those who are enlightened ... are saved in our Prayer-Meetings',[125] the Evangelicals would not willingly keep children out if their behaviour suggested they were ripe for conversion. But they were careful. Even when they were satisfied of promising behaviour, they were reluctant to let children in. Once in, however, the children sometimes became the soundest members.[126]

'Preaching kindles the fire, but Societies nurse and keep the flame alive,'[127] said Berridge. So it was that the Evangelicals, sometimes as young children, usually in youth, were nourished in the ways of their Fathers.

REFERENCES

1. *Poetical Works*, VII, p. 174.
2. Ibid. p. 133.
3. J. Everett, *Wesleyan Methodism in Manchester*, I, I, p. 157.
4. J. H. Pratt, *Eclectic Notes*, p. 201.
5. J. H. Pratt, *Remains of the Rev. R. Cecil*, pp. 273–7.
6. *Works of the Rev. Wm Jay*, Vol. XI, Preface.
7. Ibid. X, p. 514.
8. G. W. E. Russell, *The Household of Faith*, p. 241.
9. *Poetical Works*, VII, p. 42.
10. Ibid. p. 162.
11. John Pearson, *The Life of Wm Hey, Esq., F.R.S.*, pp. 298–303.
12. Venn, *Correspondence*, p. 121.
13. J. D. Walsh, Thesis: *The Yorkshire Evangelicals in the Eighteenth Century*, p. 149.
14. *Life of Henry Longden of Sheffield*, p. 154.
15. J. H. Pratt, *Eclectic Notes*, p. 392.
16. Ibid. pp. 72–5.
17. W. H. Proby, *Annals of the Low Church Party*, I, pp. 124–5
18. J. Venn, *Annals of a Clerical Family*, pp. 53–4.
19. J. C. Ryle, *Christian Leaders of the last Century*, pp. 300–1.
20. J. H. Pratt, *Eclectic Notes*, p. 74.
21. H. Venn, *Complete Duty of Man*, pp. 241–2.
22. Rev. G. Beebee, *Counsel and Warning to New Converts*.
23. J. H. Pratt, *Eclectic Notes*, p. 280.
24. L. F. Church, *Early Methodist People*, p. 224.

25. *Poetical Works*, V, p. 394.
26. *Evangelical Magazine* (1797), p. 92.
27. *Arminian Magazine* (1781), p. 57.
28. Thos. Jackson, *Recollections of my own Life and Times*, pp. 26–7.
29. *Evangelical Magazine* (1794), p. 443.
30. Rowland Hill, *Instructions for Children*, Example V.
31. Samuel Walker, *Fifty-two Sermons*, p. 140.
32. E. Sidney, *Life and Remains of the Rev. Samuel Walker*, p. 216.
33. Southey, *Life of Wesley*, II, pp. 2–3.
34. *Poetical Works*, VII, p. 165.
35. *Arminian Magazine* (1779), p. 30.
36. *Works*, I, p. 359.
37. Rowland Hill, *Instructions for Children*, Example X.
38. *Evangelical Magazine* (1793), pp. 133–8.
39. Ibid. (1794), p. 49.
40. J. H. Pratt, *Eclectic Notes*, p. 391.
41. J. Telford, *Life of Charles Wesley*, p. 266.
42. *Journal of Charles Wesley*, ed. T. Jackson, II, p. 278.
43. *Arminian Magazine* (1778), p. 475.
44. Mary Milner, *Isaac Milner*, p. 601.
45. J. Venn, *Annals of a Clerical Family*, p. 82.
46. Manuscript letter from the Venn Manuscripts Collection. Copied and given to me by Dr J. D. Walsh, of Jesus College, Oxford.
47. J. Venn, *The Life and a Selection from the Letters of the late Rev. Henry Venn*, Quotations in order, pp. 82, 273–4, 470, 265, 263–7.
48. *Evangelical Magazine* (1821), p. 227.
49. *Arminian Magazine* (1780), p. 434.
50. G. W. E. Russell, *The Household of Faith*, p. 236.
51. *Remains of T. W. Hill*, Quoted in *Johnson's England*, ed. A. S. Turberville, I, p. 359.
52. *Some Account of the Life and Writings of Mrs Trimmer*, I, p. 24.
53. L. Tyerman, *Life of Wesley*, I, p. 22.
54. *Poetical Works*, VIII, p. 393.
55. A. H. Body, Quoted in *John Wesley and Education*, pp. 73–4.
56. *Confessions of James Lackington, Bookseller*, pp. 84, 165.
57. J. W. Middleton, *An Ecclesiastical Memoir of the first four decades of the Reign of George III*, pp. 155–6.
58. *Poetical Works*, II, p. 20.
59. E. Sidney, *Life of Sir Richard Hill*, pp. 491–4.
60. H. More, *Annals*, pp. 6–9.
61. G. J. Stevenson, *History of City Road Chapel*, p. 41.
62. Henry Venn, *Correspondence*, p. 247.
63. 'At the Opening of a School in Kingswood,' *Poetical Works*, VI, p. 408.
64. A. H. Body, *John Wesley and Education*, p. 102.
65. W. H. Fitchett, *Wesley and His Century*, p. 494.
66. J. H. Whiteley, *Wesley's England*, p. 273.
67. A. H. Body, *John Wesley and Education*, p. 96.

68. L. F. Church, *Early Methodist People*, p. 236.
69. Three Old Boys, *A History of Kingswood School*, p. 15.
70. *Arminian Magazine* (1779), p. 41.
71. *An Account of the Religious and Literary Life of Adam Clarke*, ed. J. B. B. Clarke, I, p. 162.
72. *Works*, III, pp. 319–20.
73. Ibid. III, pp. 414–5.
74. Ibid. III, p. 442.
75. Ibid. III, p. 479.
76. Ibid. III, p. 147.
77. Bill-book of 1764–70, in the possession of Kingswood School.
78. *Works*, IV, p. 343.
79. Ibid. IV, p. 471.
80. L. Tyerman, *George Whitefield*, I, p. 440.
81. Ibid. p. 444.
82. Ibid. p. 440.
83. Ibid. p. 476.
84. L. Tyerman, *Wesley's Designated Successor*, pp. 477–8.
85. M. G. Jones, *Hannah More*, p. 14.
86. J. H. Whiteley, *Wesley's England*, p. 135.
87. J. W. Middleton, *An Ecclesiastical Memoir of the first four decades of the Reign of George III*, p. 203.
88. *Evangelical Magazine* (1798), p. 218.
89. J. Pearson, *The Life of Wm Hey, Esq., F.R.S.*, pp. 308–19.
90. Beilby Porteus, *A Letter to the Clergy of the Diocese of Chester concerning Sunday Schools* (2nd Edn., 1786), p. 21.
91. J. Taylor, *Robert Raikes and Northamptonshire Sunday Schools*, pp. 14–5.
92. *Evangelical Magazine* (1798), pp. 17–58.
93. M. G. Jones, *Hannah More*, p. 155.
94. H. More, *Annals*, VIII.
95. H. More, *Letters*, pp. 150–2.
96. M. G. Jones, *Hannah More*, p. 161.
97. Ibid. p. 153.
98. *Life of Henry Longden, of Sheffield*, p. 109.
99. L. Tyerman, *Life of George Whitefield*, I, p. 557.
100. J. H. Pratt, *Eclectic Notes*, p. 364.
101. E. Sidney, *Life of Rowland Hill*, p. 141.
102. Sir Leslie Stephen, *English Thought in the Eighteenth-century*, II, p. 423.
103. L. Tyerman, *Life of George Whitefield*, I, p. 50.
104. *Memoirs of Benjamin Franklin*, I, p. 85.
105. R. S. Hardy, *Life of Grimshaw*, p. 102.
106. H. Venn, *Life of Grimshaw*, p. 33.
107. E. Sidney, *Life of Rowland Hill*, pp. 265–6.
108. Thos Webster, *Sermon ... the Death of the Rev. Thos. Robinson*, p. 7.
109. Wm. Jay, *Works*, V, p. 13.
110. Sir James Stephen, *Essays in Ecclesiastical Biography*, p. 64.
111. L. Tyerman, *Life of George Whitefield*, I, p. 278.

112. *Evangelical Magazine* (1794), pp. 198–200.
113. J. H. Pratt, *Eclectic Notes*, p. 6.
114. G. J. Stevenson, *City Road Chapel, London*, pp. 84–5.
115. G. R. Balleine, *A History of the Evangelical Party*, p. 106.
116. M. G. Jones, *Hannah More*, pp. 180–1.
117. J. H. Pratt, *Eclectic Notes*, p. 6.
118. W. H. Proby, *Annals of the Low Church Party*, p. 300.
119. *Works*, II, p. 454.
120. L. Tyerman, *Life of George Whitefield*, I, p. 391.
121. *Recollections of Thomas Jackson*, pp. 26, 50.
122. G. J. Stevenson, *City Road Chapel, London*, p. 437.
123. Ibid. p. 84.
124. *Works*, III, p. 506.
125. *Life of Henry Longden of Sheffield, by Himself*, p. 48.
126. *Works*, XIII, p. 372.
127. John Berridge, *Collection of Divine Songs*, Preface.

CHAPTER V

The Matter of their Teaching

SOME EVANGELICALS considered that theology was a science too advanced for children, that it was better to imbibe its essentials little by little until the pattern emerged of its own accord. Those few who considered it appropriate failed to make it sufficiently simple, and also tended to over-stress the element of fear, presumably because the innate wickedness of children would be proof against all but the fiercest thrusts of dogma.

Rowland Hill is typical in this, and typical also in his use of evangelical clichés, an obvious danger when to avoid them would plunge him in so much more theological explanation. His treatise, *Instructions for Children*, begins with a consideration of the nature of God, and he moves swiftly on to 'the wonderful love of God in the salvation of sinners by Jesus Christ'. A simplified life of Christ follows, with various interpolations as salutary hints for the child readers. Jesus the Carpenter, for instance, tells us that 'no work should shame us, but the shameful work of sin'. The Crucifixion and Ascension as facts are well explained, but the attempt to discover their implications is less happy. 'Thus'—this is an optimistic opening, since Hill has not explained how the cause governed the effect—'the dear Redeemer lived and died to save the fallen race of sinners' and 'went again to heaven to plead the merits of his precious death for man'. This wording is hopelessly inadequate for children.

Hill's whole attitude to children is coloured by his firm hold on the Doctrine of Total Depravity. This finds its fullest expression in his sermon: 'Come, ye children, and I will show you the fear of the Lord.' The discourse begins

with 'his blessed law, which forbids us all to sin against
him', and the doctrine of Original Sin soon follows. Adam
and Eve 'being corrupted parents, their children were
corrupted also; insomuch that ... Cain was a bloody
murderer'. Yet there is a gentler side to Hill. His deep love
for children and his hard Calvinistic theory make a strange
mixture of the whole. The man who told his young readers
very clearly of their damnable nature ended his *Instructions*
beautifully: 'Very soon Jesus will come again to judgement'
and 'shall say, "Come ye blessed children of my Father,
inherit the kingdom prepared for you from the beginning
of the world".'

That this outline of theology for children remained the
approved pattern is attested by a much later Evangelical who
described the theology he was taught when a boy as th,
'Gospel Plan'—'that all mankind were utterly sinful, and
therefore in danger of hell; that God has provided deliver-
ance in the Atoning Death of Christ; and that, if only we
would accept the offer of salvation so made, we were for-
given, reconciled, and safe'.[1]

Many theological schemes could be devised to show more
fully what the Evangelicals taught their children of the ways
of God. Perhaps the simplest is the best. God, Man, the
World and Salvation are the four headings under which
their teaching will be considered here.

GOD

'Excluding the first person of the Trinity,' said R. A. Knox,
'is endemic to Methodism.'[2] This is a gross overstatement
of the truth—as fair as the accusation that the Roman
Catholics have added through the Marian Cult a fourth
Person to the Trinity. A more true criticism might have
been that the Evangelicals in general, and the Methodists in
particular, tended to make a most dangerous dichotomy
between the first two Persons of the Trinity.

The Evangelicals did not begin it. It can be traced through
the centuries in many crude systems of theology. It is only

a variation in effect of the Roman Catholic Cults of St Mary and St Anne, which are used by the ignorant to persuade God, against his better judgement, to grant the devotees' plea for the sake of the intermediaries. Charles Wesley, however, is an outspoken offender. In a most powerful hymn 'God cried out'.

> *Let Me alone,—that all My wrath*
> *   May rise, the wicked to consume:*
> *While Justice hears thy praying faith*
> *   It cannot seal the sinner's doom;*
> *My son is in My servant's prayer,*
> *And Jesus forces Me to spare.*

The mortal sinner cries—

> *Father; regard Thy pleading Son,*
> *   Accept His all-availing prayer.*[3]

This is not an isolated instance. It is based, of course, on Exodus 32, but this does not explain a similar idea in hymns intended especially for children. In 'A thought on Judgement' the child asks:

> *And must I be to judgement brought,*
> *   And answer in that day*
> *For every vain or idle thought,*
> *   And every word I say?*

The answer is yes, and only a partial qualification is made in the later—

> *My peace Thou hast already made,*
> *   While hanging on the tree;*
> *My sins He on Thy body laid,*
> *   And punish'd them in Thee*[4]

a verse which suggests that God used Jesus as a whipping-boy.

The same division of the Trinity can be found in other Evangelicals. Grimshaw's strange vision contains a strong hint of it. 'He heard ... somewhat of a conference, betwixt God the Father and the Lord Jesus Christ, concerning him and for a long time it seemed to go hard against him; for God the Father would have him to be damned ... but the Lord Jesus pleaded for him.'[5] Rowland Hill's phrase, quoted above, 'to plead the merits of his precious death', contains in its verb the same division. Again, Hill's '*Jesus* will come again to judgement' suggests that on this second occasion it will be 'come ye blessed', for God the Son is less harsh than his Father.

Here is the kernel of the dogma. God the Father is primarily the Law, and so becomes associated with Judgement, Damnation and Hell; Christ is the Gospel, and so is Love, Salvation, and Heaven. The children might well say, again with Charles Wesley, 'We from our God with horror fly' (another hymn for children) to Jesus: 'He purged our sin, He bought our peace.'[6] The idea 'and God himself is born' was certainly taught, but the stress on the teaching of the Law for children resulted in this strange division of God.

So it was that Adam Clarke 'dreaded God, and obeyed only through fear', because 'the severe creed of his Mother [a Calvinist] led her more frequently to represent the Supreme Being as a God of justice, than as the God of mercy';[7] and so it was, in all probability, that some of the later Evangelicals, through their stress on Salvation through Christ, incurred the charge of ignoring the first Person of the Trinity.

God the Father was a God of vengeance.

> *Two sinners God's just vengeance felt*
> *For telling one presumptuous lie:*
> *Dear children, learn to dread his wrath,*
> *Lest you should also sin and die.*[8]

A footnote adds: 'Here children are requested to read how Ananias and Sapphira were struck dead for telling a lie. Acts 5 to verse 12.'

His punishments sometimes seemed out of proportion to the sin. When her child of twelve months died the young mother wrote: 'O! my God, grant that this stroke may bring me and mine near to thee by repentance and faith. Sunday sins ... vain trifling, and wandering thoughts, punished by the loss of so dear an object.' Even this grief was sinful—it hinted at God being harsh. It was accordingly punished the following year by the death of a four-year-old boy. 'I felt this stroke a punishment for my great grief for the loss of my dear Frances.'[9] This second account of a loss is more wisely resigned.

No breach of God's Law was too trivial for judgement to be waived. Joseph Pearson, when a boy, fed his rabbits on a Sunday. They died.[10] It never occurred to him to doubt that God had thus punished him for his wickedness.

God often used illness, children were told, to bring His people back to Him. They should therefore rejoice at sickness.

> *Welcome, incurable disease,*
> *Whate'er my gracious God decrees*
> *My happy choice I make.*[11]

When Catherine Corbett was sixteen, 'God was pleased to stop me in my course, by sending me a severe fit of sickness',[12] for Catherine had drifted from her early piety. John Bowles was much younger when God cured him of a hasty temper. 'And now we shall see how good the Lord was in chastising this child,' the infant readers were informed. 'It was in great mercy that the Lord afflicted him with a pain in his right knee.' The child spent the remainder of his short life in pain and badly lame, but at least 'perpetual seriousness sat upon his countenance'.[13]

Such, then, was the general impression that children gained of God the Father—terrible, remote, yet frighteningly near on occasion, swift to anger and of unrelenting justness. But this was by no means all. A general impression of God was what nearly all men shared—Evangelicals expected a very particular impression also. Not only did God show a marked preference for the Protestant way of worshipping Him, but He also frequently indulged in 'Special Providences' on behalf of His evangelical flock.

All Evangelicals devoutly believed in these special interferences of God for them. Sometimes the Providences were of special mercy, as Wesley's account of the fire at Kingswood,[14] the miraculous escapes from death of Matthias Joyce[15] or Adam Clarke[16] on whose behalf it is claimed, by a curious logic, 'Had he not been designed for matters of great and high importance, it is not likely ... he could have survived this accident'. Sometimes they were Providences of Judgement, such as God's wrath at Popery, which resulted, according to Tyerman,[17] in the Portuguese earthquake; or His wrath against Race-Meetings, which were rained off at Haworth through the efficacy of Grimshaw's prayer.[18] Sometimes the Providences are remarkably trivial, such as Silas Told's insistence that being thrown out of a wood by a dog 'was the Lord's doing',[19] or, to quote an extreme example, Huntington's certainty in *God the Guardian of the Poor and the Bank of Faith* that the Lord sent him a pair of breeches, that a dog brought him mutton to eat, and fish died at night in a pond on purpose to be eaten by him in the morning. The most extreme claim of all is an ambiguously worded one in the *Methodist Magazine* of October 1804, which strongly implies a raising from the dead.

That much of this is the fruit of the famous evangelical superstition cannot be denied. It is most difficult to argue about it, however, for God alone knows how His Providence is used. What is certain is that children found no difficulty in believing even the most extraordinary of these Special Providences. Childhood, now as then, is a gullible time, and the various 'Anecdotes' of the *Evangelical Magazine*, however improbable, however ludicrous, would be readily accepted by the child readers.

Blended with this belief in Special Providences, and an almost inevitable corollary of it, is a kind of fatalism.

Though textual proof of it being taught to children is lacking, there is an underlying feeling in most of the few extant writings of children themselves, and notably in Mary Gilbert's *Journal*, that whatever happens is the will of God, but a will so inscrutable as to be incomprehensible; that men are completely at the mercy of a Being whose Nature (here again is the division of the Trinity, for this Being is God the Father alone) is completely unknown, and whose very actions, at least humanly speaking, appear arbitrary.

And fatalistic also, in this case explicit, was the demand made on children to submit to the decrees of God. Resignation was taught. There is inconsistency between precept and example here, but very understandably so. Though Charles Wesley could cheerfully write 'Thanksgiving to God for his Disappointments', and even 'A Mother's Thanksgiving for the Death of her Child', since the child would be

> *Beyond the range of fiends removed,*
> *Took from a world he never loved,*

when his own son embraced Popery the agonized hymn shows little resignation.[20] Yet perhaps there is no inconsistency in Charles's own mind; the boy was certainly considered to have suffered a fate worse than death, and even the strange decrees of God could hardly make Popery acceptable.

Joy in God, except where the joy rested in Christ's sacrifice, was rare among the Evangelicals. God the Father for them was hardly a Being to inspire Joy. He inspired awe, but the awe that is composed more of terror than love. Indeed, many of the Evangelicals never found joy at all. Even among the Arminians, where Wesley prescribed it as a proof of the divine indwelling, a few found only peace. Children who found joy usually found it (according to their elders and betters) in doing what they should. Until their second birth, children could find happiness only in the paths of duty.

Happy beyond description he
Who in the paths of piety
Loves from his birth to run:
Its ways are ways of pleasantness,
And all its paths are joy and peace,
And heaven on earth begun.[21]

The Third Person of the Trinity received scant attention by children. The very difficulty of the idea of the Holy Spirit makes this natural. As far as the understanding of children was concerned, the Evangelicals probably (and reasonably) considered that it was easier to believe in the presence of Christ still working in the world than to baffle infant minds with a doctrine that could wait for mature years.

Rowland Hill, however, confusingly does his duty and informs the children that: 'By his intercession, God the Holy Spirit, again came down and dwelt upon this earth, and he is to be with us always, even to the end of the world: by his grace our hearts are to be changed. If you, dear children, have his grace your hearts will be changed also; you will hate sin.' Few children could make much of this.

If the children of the Evangelicals feared God the Father, and knew little of the Holy Spirit, at least they had a very clear idea of the world to come. In an age when the literal inspiration of the Bible was unquestioned, and among influences where the Bible was the centre of faith and the world to come much more important than the present world, it was natural that the children should have been steeped in an exact knowledge of heaven and hell, largely culled from the book of Revelation.

Heaven for children was a very musical place. 'There will be no striking a wrong string, no singing a wrong note, there we shall play on a 10-stringed instrument. O that will be brave!'[22] There appeared to be variety in instruments as well as harmony; one child is to have 'a little trumpet',[23] another 'His golden lyre',[24] All angels, especially cherubs, will be musicians.

Clothes also vary. The most detailed are—

> *In garb angelic drest;*
>
> *A royal coronet*
> *Upon his head they place;*
>
> *They robe him in the milk-white vest.*[25]

while others have to be content with a mere 'white robe'.[26]

Rowland Hill was exceedingly clever in conveying a visual picture of heaven. One of his pious children,[27] near to death, had already seen heaven in anticipation, with 'the heavenly host all standing round the throne' and 'Mr W——, a good Christian, lately deceased', among them. When another child dies,[28] Hill explained in a matter-of-fact way, precisely as he had told the rest, how the child was carried to heaven by an angel, and an illustration shows it.

Hell was even more fully described than Heaven, and certainly referred to more often. The Evangelical catechism 'For Children of Tender Years' ran:

Q. What sort of a place is Hell?
A. A dark and bottomless pit, full of fire and brimstone.
Q. How will the wicked be punished there?
A. Their bodies will be tormented by fire.

Rowland Hill's happy knack of impressing images served him as well with Hell as with Heaven: 'All Liars shall have their part in the lake which burneth with fire and brimstone: and how grievously they are tormented you will see in the picture.' The picture, though a poor one, would give to the child-reader a frightening idea of his possible destination.

A Calvinist theology precludes any idea of Purgatory, so one large section of evangelical children was taught to expect Heaven or Hell immediately after death. Judgement is so perfunctory in some accounts as to have been left out altogether, again a natural omission in Calvinist doctrine. Either the child awaited his approaching dissolution with

'Come, my dear Redeemer, come send the fiery chariot, and fetch my longing soul!' and encouraged his brothers and sisters with a pointing finger and the words, 'O then you will go down, down, down into torment and misery!'[29] Or, being wayward, he prepared himself to fall into the

> *pit beneath the grave,*
> *The same into which Satan fell:*
> *God made it in his holy wrath,*
> *And call'd the horrid dungeon, Hell.*[30]

The same breath that might have been used in singing God's praises would be pressed into baser uses:

> *While they enjoy his heavenly love*
> *Must I in torments dwell?*
> *And howl (while they sing hymns above),*
> *And blow the flames of Hell?*[31]

There can be little doubt that it was in part these strong visual impressions that led to the agonies of fear which so many young Evangelicals suffered; the literal aspects of some of their theology would be certain to cause terror in sensitive minds. So it was that a man could write: 'From 10 or 11 years of age, I was exceedingly distrest. I generally saw, as I thought, Hell before me,'[32] and another man recorded that in early youth he saw an angel 'glancing at me with his piercing eyes, and waving his hand: he pronounced those awful words, "There is no room in heaven for such as you!" '[33]

But meanwhile, though the children's eyes were fixed heavenwards, or gazed in terror at the awful prospect of hell, for a while, at least, they had to come to terms with themselves.

MAN

THE NATURE OF MAN

'And now, dear children, let me see if I cannot show you somewhat of the wickedness of your own hearts ... for all children are born in sin, and therefore cannot be saved without his grace and mercy.'[34]

Children were left in no doubt about their corrupted condition. The Doctrine of Original Sin was held by all Evangelicals and brought them much abuse. In 1756 the Archbishop of Canterbury called it 'wicked and blasphemous' and twisted the doctrine to make it assert 'men are by nature devils'. The Evangelicals were unimpressed, however, and taught the doctrine early. Adam's sin, children were told, brought about the fall of man; so came death, sin, and sorrow into the world and so all succeeding generations, except through the mediation of Christ, are subject to God's just vengeance for that sin. Urgent was it, therefore, that children should avail themselves of Christ's sacrifice as soon as possible.

The Evangelicals did not shrink from the logic of their own doctrine. Each knew himself

> *By nature and by practice too,*
> *A wretched slave to sin,*[35]

and each knew that the sufferings of children were not necessarily for their own misdeeds, but for man's first sin. Even if the child is in a state of baptismal innocence, God's vengeance on Adam's pride may still strike her:

> *Hear her help-imploring groan,*
> *Pain'd with sorrows not her own,*
> *Bruised, alas, for our offence*
> *Save her suffering innocence!*[36]

Even toothache—the logic is clear—is the fruit of 'guilt original we own', as Charles Wesley carefully pointed out in his hymn, 'For a child cutting his teeth'.

And if children must suffer for sins not their own, they certainly inherited the predisposition to vileness that was their birthright. Fletcher was a man of great gentleness towards children, yet he was never blind to their corruptness. 'How excessively foolish are the plays of children!' he wrote. 'How full of mischief and cruelty the sports of boys! How vain, foppish, and frothy the joys of young people!'[37]

On the question of Depravity the Evangelicals were divided. The Calvinists, inferring it from the Doctrine of Original Sin, called it Total and gave it centrality, for all else in their system logically followed; Irresistible Grace and Election were inescapable necessities if the human will was so corrupt that it could not even grope towards God. Wesley, asserting man's free will, yet admitting Original Sin, steered skilfully between the Scylla of Calvinism and the Charybdis of Semi-Pelagianism by his doctrine of Prevenient Grace, refusing Total Depravity, but asserting universal depravity, universal salvation.

It is doubtful if any children were called upon to appreciate such theological niceties, but it is possible that the sterner, Calvinistic view, taking so low a view of human nature and so high a view of the power of sin, made for an even more repressive scheme of training than the fractionally milder Arminian one. At least for the Arminians some particle of God remained in man.

Totally depraved or universally depraved, all evangelical children knew they were, in Rowland Hill's words,

> *Born a poor sinful helpless babe;*
> *Born but to weep and groan and die,*

and that they were of the earth, earthy, and so must remain until grace had refined their wicked hearts. Their deep sinfulness was the first lesson that the children learned. It is no wonder that most of them feared hell more than they sought heaven.

Even in their depraved state, the children were expected to shun the devil's lures. While those under evangelical influence from birth should be able to avoid the grosser sins, this did not necessarily apply to child converts, and sin was considered so radical in children that even under the best possible influences (at Kingswood, for instance) the devil might creep in.

Consequently, there are a number of echoes of Watts's hymn 'Against Lying' written for children—

> *Then let me always watch my lips,*
> *Lest I be struck to death and hell,*
> *Since God a book of reckoning keeps*
> *For every lie that children tell—*

and it is apparently necessary to caution children against even worse sins:

> *While others early learn to swear,*
> *And curse, and lie, and steal.*

The subtlest sin, the greatest proof of the mark of the beast, is the sin of pride, and children were especially warned against it. So many were

> *With hellish emulation fired,*
> *They lust to be caress'd, admired,*
> *And pamper'd with applause.*[38]

Girls were even more liable to the sin than boys.

> *Ah, dire effect of female pride!*
> *The poison spreads throughout our veins,*
> *In all our sex the evil reigns,*
> *The arrogant offence.*[39]

If conversion were too long delayed, then the children were warned of the awful consequences. Small sins would become greater until the graceless infant would become notorious for

> *His wild disorder'd ways,*
> *His enmity to things Divine,*
> *His league with hell, his feasts with swine,*
> *His total want of grace.*[40]

His fate was then certain. He would

> *Feel the worm that never dies*
> *In endless flames to dwell.*[41]

In the early days of the Evangelical Revival, class-consciousness was an implicit assumption and therefore never mentioned. Later—for what reason or combination of reasons it is difficult to say—many of the Evangelicals made the implicit explicit. Perhaps because the movement was no longer persecuted, but firmly established, and in large part settled as a 'middle-class' movement; perhaps also because their religion had brought them wealth in its train, and with it a *'nouveau riche'* temperament, the followers of Wesley tended to forget that the world was their parish. The fusion of charitable actions and evangelical zeal, noted earlier, somehow produced an unfortunate attitude by some of the Evangelicals to the poorer classes outside their influence. When, through their acts of charity the later Evangelicals met the outcasts of England, like their predecessors they were shocked, and a new sin was added to the catalogue of infant failings—vulgarity.

> *Immodest speeches, songs obscene,*
> *Teach them to shun and hate;*
> *With what is vulgar, low, or mean,*
> *In language or in gait.*[42]

Quite how one can be 'vulgar' in 'gait' I do not know, but it is an interesting thought! Typical also of this attitude is the comment on the Squire's expostulation to the naughty boy at Sunday-school: 'It was very kind and Christian-like, on the part of that good gentleman, to take pains to convert a poor, ragged worthless boy.'[43]

If the Evangelicals should be considered inconsistent in demanding such a high standard of goodness from such vile children, then they could defend themselves by pointing out how contemptuously they regarded 'mere morality'. In fact they were not so scornful of works that they carried the theory to its fantastic logical conclusion as some of the Moravians did. Though children were taught that good works would avail them nothing, and that by faith alone they could be saved, yet as far as behaviour was concerned, 'mere morality' was not bad, but it was not enough.

A very high proportion of evangelical children sought God first through observance of the Law, and of course they failed. In their later spiritual history they tended to look back at this period and marvel at their obtuseness and the sad waste of time. There is good reason to suppose, however, that this stage was an essential part of their spiritual development. Typical of girls carefully nurtured in the evangelical faith is this description: 'Her appearance was interesting, and her address genteel. Her mind also was naturally lively, her temper remarkably sweet, and her conduct strictly moral.... These excellences left this young lady, as they do many of her sex and age, totally destitute of spiritual religion.'[44] Nor, the children were told, could natural man achieve more, and much more was needful. Sin was paramount; only Christ could break its power. A second birth was necessary, and the birth-pangs could be, and should be, anticipated. The children must prepare.

THE DUTY OF MAN

'And now let poor unhappy children stop and consider what a state they are in,' recommended Rowland Hill, for the first duty of the would-be Christian was Self-Examination.

Wesley used a scheme of it as early as his Holy Club days, and it is interesting that he recommended it ever afterwards, even though it belonged to his pre-conversion period. This scheme demanded a life of remarkable holiness, which he lived. For instance, the question, 'Have I every hour prayed for Humility, Faith, Hope, Love, and the particular virtue of the day?' requires a near saint to give an affirmation.

All the Evangelicals observed it. Venn, Stonhouse and Hervey write at length of its efficacy, Stonhouse recommending it especially for children, and Walker of Truro was so well known for it that his biographer wondered if 'Methodism' meant 'self-scrutiny'.

It was expected of children as it was of adults. Wesley never tired of urging children to keep diaries of their spiritual condition, and that the function of these diaries was a form of self-examination is clear from the few examples that survive. Many Evangelicals who later recorded their pre-conversion condition tell how important a part in their experience self-examination played. Thomas Olivers, for instance, almost lost his reason through it, and Hester Ann Rogers, another famous Methodist, found little joy in her religion because from childhood she never ceased to examine herself before God. Many child heroes and heroines spent their years of infancy weeping over their sinful condition, urged to it by relatives and friends. It was a commonplace among evangelical correspondents to ask only of the condition of the other's soul, and to send news only of the spiritual condition of the writer. It is no wonder, when one considers the normal correspondence of Wesley with women like Ruth Hall and Sarah Ryan, that a girl of thirteen whom he examined spiritually was in great pain.[45] If self-examination could lead to insanity, examination of a sinner by a saint might well be painful.

It was perhaps inevitable that a theology which despised 'works' in theory (though doing so many good works in practice) should lean to this dangerous method of religious discipline. A constant searching of their own motives by children, a constant self-absorption, a conviction that to relax spiritually for one moment of time might lead to perdition, all these things were aids by which saints might reach heaven, but as easily snares by which sinners might fall to despair and even suicide. Too many accounts, as will be seen, show the morbid depths to which this practice brought its disciples. Yet as surely, and this is a constant mystery of some dangerous evangelical practices, it brought others to a relationship with God that perhaps no other method could have achieved. A sense of sin is a necessity of Christianity, and it can only come by looking within.

The Evangelicals, as a second step on the ladder to

70	GLORY
	Dismission from the body.
60	Desiring to depart, to be with Christ.
	Patience in tribulation.
	Glorying in the Cross.
50	Ardent love to the souls of men.
	Following hard after God.
	Deadness to the world by the Cross of Christ.
40	Love of God shed abroad in the heart.
	Frequent approach to the Lord's Table.
	Meetings for prayer and experience.
30	Delight in the people of God.
	Looking to Jesus.
20	Love of God's house and word.
	Vain company wholly dropp'd.
	Daily perusal of the Bible with prayer.
10	Evangelical light.
	Retirement for prayer and meditation.
	Concern for the soul. Alarm.
0—	INDIFFERENCE
	Family worship only on Sunday evenings.
	Private prayer frequently omitted.
	Family religion wholly declined.
10	Levity in conversation.
	Fashions, however expensive or indecent, adopted.
20	Luxurious entertainments.
	Free association with carnal company.
30	The Theatre, Vauxhall, Ranelagh, etc.
	Frequent parties of pleasure. House of God forsaken.
	Much wine, spirits, etc.
40	Love of Novels, etc.
	Scepticism—Private prayer totally declined.
	Deistical company prized.
50	Parties of pleasure on the Lord's Day.
	Masquerades, Drunkenness—Adultery.
	Profaneness, lewd songs.
60	Infidelity—jesting at religion.
	Sitting down in the chair of the scorner.
70	Death.
	PERDITION

Heaven, prescribed 'seriousness'. It is almost always opposed to 'levity' or 'trifling', and means a constant awareness of one's sinful condition and of the sacrifice of Christ. Charles Wesley wrote 'A Hymn for Seriousness'. Children were judged in spiritual progress by growth of 'seriousness'. In part, of course, it was a negative quality: it meant an absence of animal spirits, an avoidance of trivial conversation; in part it was positive, and the positive signs in children were desire to read the Bible, to ask religious questions, to indulge in self-examination, in all ways to consider eternity and abandon temporal interests.

Children were not left without guides to their spiritual progress. The *Evangelical Magazine* in 1797 published an article on 'Signs of a Living or Growing Christian'. The first sign was, 'When your chief delight is with the saints, especially them that excel in virtue'. Three years later the same magazine published an even more useful guide: 'The Spiritual Barometer: or, a scale of the progress of Sin and of Grace' (see page 147).

This remarkable guide shows just what growing 'seriousness' entailed. Just above 'Indifference' are the stages through which the child must pass to eventual 'Glory'. The most sinister of these is 'Alarm'.

'Come, ye children, hearken unto me, and I will teach you the fear of the Lord' was the common text for children's sermons. Few of the preachers, however, explained that a fear synonymous with terror was a necessary step towards God. Yet their teaching to children made it unavoidable. 'That there was an unhealthy element of fear', writes L. F. Church with reference to early Methodist religious instruction, 'must be at once admitted.'[46] While Dr Johnson and Bishop Butler were both terrified of death, they were reluctant to admit it. Only the Evangelicals deliberately used fear of death as an educational process, and wrote, themselves having passed that way, that it was a preconversion necessity. Three consecutive verses of one of Charles Wesley's hymns for children begin:

> *And am I born to die?*
>
> *What will become of me?*
>
> *How shall I leave my tomb?*[47]

The high infant mortality rate was pressed into service.

> *There is an hour when I must die,*
> *Nor do I know how soon 'twill come:*
> *A thousand children, young as I,*
> *Are called by death to hear their doom.*[48]

Every method of painting the horrors of hell was a legitimate way of frightening children into a fear which might lead to conversion. It was such a system that William James in his *Varieties of Religious Experience*, called 'morbidness', contrasting it with the 'healthy-mindedness' of less severe theologies, and in extreme cases the morbidness proved fatal. Morgan, a member of the Holy Club at Oxford, starved himself to death in the grip of religious melancholia; Mark Bond lived a life of pious misery, another melancholiac; John Reed's terrors exceeded the others—he believed, like Bunyan, that he had committed the unforgivable sin.

Yet it was through this same process of fear that many of the Evangelicals, as children, first approached Conversion, and it was natural that in their turn they should use a method which had been proven successful. Most of Wesley's Preachers passed through the stage; the Countess of Huntingdon's conversion followed soon after an encounter with 'a youthful corpse',[49] Fletcher's first religious thoughts came from a maid threatening him with Hell.[50] When John Nelson's 'flesh crept on his bones'[51] at reading Revelation 20 he was near conversion, and Thomas Scott reached the same stage only after he was 'disquieted with apprehensions of the wrath of an offended God'.[52]

Such cases were relatively mild. '*Timor mortis conturbat me*' is normal. The more remarkable cases, typically evangelical and extreme of that kind if by no means rare, were the obsessional ones which approached madness, but, unlike those of Morgan, Bond and Reed, passed through the pathological state of terror into eventual happiness by the way of conversion.

'When God brought Israel out of Egypt', wrote John Newton, 'He did not lead them to Canaan by the shortest way, but round by the wilderness, to humble and prove them, and show them what was in their hearts. . . . Thus we usually pass through a long train of trying exercises; we mourn over our own broken promises, and weary ourselves with vain and perplexing contrivances. . . .'[53] These 'trying exercises', therefore, were expected, and took the form of visions, nightmares, deep depression, and abnormal fears. Grimshaw himself felt 'urged to blaspheme',[54] an experience Bunyan had suffered before him. Almost all Wesley's Preachers had at least two of the experiences listed above, usually in their early teens. In the chronicles of these men phrases such as 'terrified with thoughts of death', 'horror seized me', and 'conscience tortured with fear and alarm' are commonplace.[55] Perhaps the most interesting case is Joseph Cownley's. He was afraid to answer a question lest, unwittingly, he should not speak the truth and so would be damned. Several found their lives an almost intolerable burden, several contemplated suicide. Nor were those particular experiences confined to one small group of Methodists. Later Adam Clarke,[56] as a child of six, had similar experiences, Ann Simpson,[57] at sixteen 'saw Satan in a hideous form, just ready to devour me', and several of Rowland Hill's pious children suffered in this way at varying ages.

'Read also often Treatises of death.' The Evangelicals gave the children ample opportunity. They made a fashion of the death-bed and encouraged children to cultivate it assiduously.

Part of the reason, no doubt, was the very high infant mortality rate. Children could expect death in the house at frequent intervals. The rate of dying under five years of age between 1730 and 1749 was 74·5 per 100 births. Part also was the current cult of the tomb.

The Evangelicals had no monopoly of the macabre. This was the age of Young's *Night Thoughts*, Blair's *Grave*, and Gray's *Elegy*. At this period the Neo-Gothic Revival was beginning, mildly at first with Horace Walpole's *Castle of Otranto*, but later it was to become the horror school of 'Monk' Lewis and Mrs Radcliffe. Hervey, author of *Meditations Among the Tombs*, was an Evangelical, but his work did not differ markedly from men of other religious persuasions or none at all. 'O ye timorous souls, that are terrified at the sound of the passing bell: that turn pale at the sight of an opened grave; and can scarce behold a coffin or a skull, without a shuddering horror; ye that are in bondage to the grisly tyrant, and tremble at the shaking of his iron rod; cry mightily to the Father of your spirits, for faith in his dear Son.'[58] Only the last five words suggest the author's religious convictions. Even so solid a pillar of evangelical correctness as the *Evangelical Magazine* occasionally published work which had more of the Neo-Gothic than the Christian.

> *Attend, ye fair, ye thoughtless and ye gay!*
> *For Myra died upon her nuptial day!*
> *The grave, cold bridegroom, clasped her in its arms,*
> *And the worm rioted upon her charms.*[59]

But the Evangelicals, whatever their debt to a current fashion of graveyard literature, adapted it to their own ends and made some aspects of it peculiarly theirs.

A very large number of funeral hymns was written by Charles Wesley, all evangelical literature abounded in accounts of death-beds, and children were taught to read them and, if necessary, emulate the piety of those who had so triumphantly achieved 'dismission from the body'. Attendance at death-beds—both before and after the death —and at funerals was considered very important. Cornelius Winter as a boy 'attended funerals till I could repeat the burial service by rote'.[60] Last words of the departing were treasured up and often used in a Memoir. The 'last words' not infrequently covered several pages. As Charles Wesley put it,

Without a groan the Christian *dies!*
But not without a word.[61]

If 'last words' of a pious nature were not forthcoming, and particularly when there was doubt concerning the final destination of the person dying, the godly gathered round to persuade him into a 'heavenly frame'. The persuasion some-times lacked tact. Henry Longden asked a dying man who assured him he would soon be in heaven: 'Have you a scrip-tural foundation for your hope?'[62]

The godly were particularly assiduous in their question-ing of children. 'When she first sickened for death, her mother asked her whether she thought she would die, and go to the Lord,' wrote Rowland Hill about Anna Shipway, one of his pious children. In other cases relatives called daily to enjoy the assurance of heaven by the dying child. It is impossible to know how often they were disappointed, for such cases would not be recorded. It seems likely, however, that the intense questioning of the children, who would be in a weak condition, anxious to please, and had at least as great hopes of heaven as their visitors, would usually have the desired result.

Wesley's own death (a painting of which is in an ante-room of Wesley's Chapel) had all the trappings that the Evangelicals loved. A large company was gathered; they sang hymns together; Wesley himself was assured of heaven, and urged his followers on; the atmosphere was triumphant. Most significantly, young James Rogers, about four, was pushed to the front of the company and, together with an old gentleman holding an ear-trumpet, who was privileged because of this handicap, had the best view of all.

Death-beds for Evangelicals were not sentimental, as with the lovers of the macabre. Wedded to evangelical relig-ion death-beds became educational and, especially with regard to children, they became the ideal places for religious instruction.

'The state of your mind when you die', Thomas Wood told children, 'must determine your place on the other side death.'[63] Death mattered more to the Evangelicals than life, and logically so. The earth they despised; to heaven they aspired. If all was well spiritually, then death was the end of the misery of existence on earth, and the beginning of bliss in heaven. 'The desire of a religious death', wrote Hanway, 'is of equal moment as a religious life, and a natural consequence.'[64] Nothing could have been more reasonable. So it was that the children were urged to see and to study as many departing saints as possible. It would whet their own appetites for heaven. And it could conquer the terrors of death. 'To disarm the king of terrors of every appearance of horror, and to welcome his Summons as a call from a vain and miserable world to a world of endless and unspeakable felicity, is the sole property of a firm faith.'[65] And there was always the hope that words made holy by the imminence of death would urge on the tardy young Evangelical to heaven; 'The words of departing saints are precious. They convince, and they encourage.'[66]

That the children were influenced by the lesson of the death-bed is certain. Henry Longden was fortunate enough to observe two strikingly different ones in childhood, and assures posterity: 'I became decided and fixed in my judgement and in my choice of religion as the one thing needful, by being providentially an eyewitness of the awful death of a sinner, and the happy exit of a saint of God.'[67] Whitefield prized the understanding of a child when he told, in a funeral sermon, how 'a noble lady' had lost a daughter and wept. 'Mamma,' asked a younger sister, 'is God Almighty dead, you cry so?' The child begged a glove which the Mother later requested. The child returned it with the words: 'Mamma! Shall I cry because you have taken back your glove? And shall you cry because God has taken back my sister?'[68] This child had profited from the death-bed of her sister precisely as the Evangelicals wished.

Modern taste is often revolted at children being pushed

near death-beds and taken to funerals. It is considered morbid. Yet one may well doubt if it is not wiser, and certaily more natural, than elaborate arrangements to keep children away, and stories of 'Granny's gone to sleep'. And there were two good reasons for it, even apart from evangelical belief in its educational powers. In the first place, as has been mentioned, it would have been impossible in the second half of the eighteenth century to keep children away from the presence of death, and in the second place it is very doubtful if their experiences of death had the harrowing effect we imagine. Martha More wrote to her more famous sister to tell Hannah of the death and funeral of Mrs Baker, which two hundred children attended, and 'sobbed a suitable hymn over the grave. When we got the children into the great room . . . I said a great deal as well as I could and I wrung their little hearts; for I knew but too well, that the world and young blood would make an excellent sponge to wipe out, full soon, the awful business of the day'.[69] Martha was probably right.

The last duty of the children of the Evangelicals was to desire death. While Charles Wesley has ten hymns in a section 'Desiring Death' and another, specifically for children, which asks God—

> *O take us away*
> *In the morn of our day,*
> *And let us no longer in misery stay*—[70]

one tends to consider such writings, and there are many such examples, if not poetic licence, at least writings which only saints could sing. Yet it was expected of all. The Spiritual Barometer, quoted above, rates 'Desiring to depart, to be with Christ', as the highest point of holiness. There are striking examples of this desire in older saints, the best authenticated of which is Henry Venn's case, for the doctor told his daughter Jane: 'Madam, your father would have died a fortnight ago if it had not been for joy at dying.'[71] Nor are examples of children desiring death uncommon.

Some appear to have ulterior motives for the wish, like Martha Hall, who longed to follow her sister and died piously at ten years of age.[72] Some death-wishes appear to be the pious thoughts of friends. There is little ring of authenticity in the bald, 'She had no relish for the perishing trifles of this life—and earnestly desired "to be dissolved and be with Christ".'[73] But other accounts, and notably Rowland Hill's, appear perfectly genuine. Wesley vouches for one small boy who was 'longing to be with Christ' but—and in the light of the death-bed fashion this is most significant—'was detained here a little longer, that he might witness "a good confession" in death as well as in life'.[74]

The fullest case of a child desiring death, and one which demonstrates well the evangelical attitude towards death is that of Elizabeth Radder,[75] who died in 1788, when she was fifteen. She had shown a longing for death very early. 'The Sabbath after my Aunt's decease, the two young friends desired to see her corpse.' Elizabeth was then about twelve. 'The two friends used to spend their evenings frequently in the churchyard, sitting on the grave of a pious young woman, who died last year; and there conversing together on the concerns of another world; and, as she told me on her sick bed, "Many mournful and many joyful hours have we spent there".' When Elizabeth lay dying, Janeway was read to her. 'Oh,' she said, 'I shall never experience such a death-bed as these sweet children did.' But she did.

In this account, the child appears to have developed through the specified evangelical channels—corpse-viewing, grave-yards, accounts of pious deaths—to the highest wish to which she could aspire, the wish to 'depart, to be with Christ'.

> Come, to the house of mourning come,
> The house of serious, solemn joy,[76]

wrote Charles Wesley. But the reason for a house of mourning being a joyful one was only clear to children if they viewed the world aright.

THE WORLD

THE NATURE OF THE WORLD

'Young people', wrote Hannah More, in one of her tracts, 'are apt to imagine that the world is full of pleasure and enjoyment.' The Evangelicals taught children the opposite. The world, on the contrary, was an evil place. Man's environment was as wicked as his own heart.

> *Foolish, ignorant, and blind*
> *Is sinful, short-lived man;*
> *All which in the world we find*
> *Is perishing and vain.*[77]

Children were therefore taught to shun worldly vanities and consider the world to come. Implicit in the teaching was the idea that the earth was only a testing-place for heaven, and that the delights of the world were placed there by the devil, in order to ensnare mankind. Death was release from the misery of life. 'If I could be sensible what these persons were doing at the moment they put me into my coffin', wrote Adam of Wintringham, 'it would be one of the most agreeable sensations I have ever known.'[78] Charles Wesley expresses his horror of the world even more strongly.

> *Exposed I long have been*
> *In this bleak vale of tears,*
> *Midst scenes of vanity and sin*
> *Consumed my threescore years:*
> *I turn my face aside,*
> *Sick of beholding more,*
> *And wish the latest storm to' outride,*
> *And reach the happy shore.*[79]

The longer the children survived, therefore, the greater the sum of this misery must be. If old age could only regret its survival, even youth was not soon enough to die for an Evangelical. A young Minister wrote his impressions of life two days before he died. The *Evangelical Magazine* of 1796 printed it approvingly. 'It cheers me to find this earthly tabernacle, in which I groan, being burdened, wasting, reeling, and ready to be dissolved. . . . Is there any thing worth living for?'

'No,' the Evangelicals could have answered; 'nothing.' Best of all would it be for children if they never reached maturity to become corrupted by the world. As his children died, William Hey visited each coffined corpse on the morning of the funeral and 'above all, he gave thanks that the child was delivered from the vanities and miseries of this evil world'.[80]

Eighteenth-century life might well have seemed abhorrent to the Evangelicals. Disease and death were the common lot, much commoner than now. Everywhere they saw 'Vanity Fair'. Poverty, drunkenness and disorder were all about them. What they endured they did not wish their children to share. How happy the children would be, they reasoned, to escape the miseries of life and attain heaven without struggling through the snares of Satan for three score years and ten.

Many children understood the lesson. Like Charlotte Brontë, they could tell their parents the best way of spending time: 'By laying it out in preparation for a happy eternity.'[81]

One would not expect Evangelicals to teach their children by Natural Religion—it would appear to clash with their theories of the vileness of the world. In fact, there is no clash; the world as God made it is a manifestation of Him: it is man who has corrupted it. Nevertheless, possibly because any praise of God's world might be mistaken for praise of man's world, an appeal to natural religion is rare. Charles Wesley hints at it once or twice—

> I see His beauty in the flower;
> To shade my walks, and deck my bower—[82]

and John Wesley suggests it in his sermon 'On Family Religion', but most of the Evangelicals consider it too dangerous an argument to use. They laboured rather to teach the wickedness of man in the world, and bent all their energies to train children to be 'in the world, yet not of the world'. How difficult this was they knew from their own experiences. Almost every activity of man's world had to be proscribed to keep the children untainted and fit for heaven.

THOU SHALT NOT

Blake surely had the Evangelicals in mind when he wrote 'The Garden of Love'.

> *And the gates of this Chapel were shut*
> *And 'Thou shalt not' writ over the door:*
> *So I turned to the Garden of Love*
> *That so many sweet flowers bore;*
> *And I saw it was filled with graves,*
> *And tomb-stones where flowers should be;*
> *And Priests in black gowns were walking their rounds,*
> *And binding with briars my joys and desires.*

This is a fair picture of Evangelicalism as it must have appeared to some children. Until the happiness of religion, until the joy of conversion was theirs, then children must have felt that life was largely a list of forbidden fruits. Nor did the teaching deny this: indeed, it affirmed it. There could be no joy except in God, and only through the mediation of Christ. All other joy was sinful. To seek 'happiness in the world'—a phrase of deepest condemnation—was to befriend the devil.

Must there be no joy? Wesley puzzled over the problem in his pre-conversion days at Oxford, passed the problem to his parents, and received a different answer from each. In the end his own experience gave him the answer. He knew no joy until his 'heart became strangely warmed' and he was converted. But he could offer no joy to the unconverted. Children would have to wait.

Inevitably this gloomy side of evangelical doctrine suggested a comparison with Puritanism, and Evangelicals shared at least this much with some of the old Puritans—a distrust of any joy that was not purely religious. Isaac Milner, by nature gay, had to check himself continually against 'a tendency to the comic',[83] and children had to check themselves also. The Rev. Winter's third son 'discovered a gaiety of temper which afforded some concern to his venerable parent; but his last illness was sanctified'.[84]

The Evangelicals all agreed that worldliness was to be shunned, but there were inconsistencies about what was and what was not allowed. Wesley wrote against powdering of hair, cards, dancing, theatres, and tobacco. Whitefield allowed 'Innocent Diversions' only, but had difficulty in deciding relative innocence, and on another occasion blames himself for reading 'Plays, *Spectators*, Pope's *Homer*, and such-like trifling books'.[85] A Miss Newman tells her friend she looks back with pleasure on the hours she spent 'acquiring a little knowledge of the Hebrew tongue with a kind of satisfaction' for it would 'be of advantage to me in preparing for the world to come', but she looks back in dismay at the time wasted in 'music, drawing and the French language'.[86] Yet Hannah More taught French and music as well as Italian and dancing at her school. There were no absolute rules.

Wesley tried to sum it all up: 'In one word, be any thing, but a Trifler: a Trifler with God and your own soul.' Diversions were in order, then, provided they did not come between God and the soul. 'Perpetual seriousness' (a phrase beloved of Rowland Hill) was the doorway to heaven.

Yet although this summing-up would have been acceptable to all, the Evangelicals loved to systematize, and children in particular needed a clear code of behaviour. So it was that Proby was able to say—unfairly, but understandably—that 'the works which evidenced a Low Churchman's faith were of a negative character'.[87]

Outward appearance proclaimed, or should proclaim, the heart within. Hence evangelical concern over dress. Wesley, himself always faultlessly neat, warned his followers of the dangers of concern over dress. It 'engenders pride', it 'breeds and increases vanity', it 'tends to beget anger', it 'tends to create and inflame lust', it is opposite to 'being adorned with good works', and it acts against 'inward holiness'. Though Wesley also observed 'slovenliness is no part of religion' many leading Evangelicals were noted for extreme shabbiness, a fault which might well seem a virtue to their congregations.

Women, naturally, were considered more prone to err in matters of dress. Wesley condemned 'elephantine hats or bonnets—those scandals of female modesty'. In an age when children dressed like their parents, girls little more than ten years old were liable also to appear in fantastic hair styles, rings, ear-rings, and ornamentations, all abhorrent in evangelical eyes. Most abhorrent of all, perhaps, was the fashion of wearing very low-cut dresses and omitting the scarf which should be worn above it to cover the breasts. One writer fumes against the practice. 'Many women, who, a little while since, shone forth among the loveliest of their sex, are now dressed in their shrouds, because, in an evil hour, they laid aside those parts of their apparel, which health, as well as decency, forbade them to relinquish.'[88]

From the cradle onwards simplicity in dress was essential. Hannah More argues against finery for the infant at a baptism 'because Christ gave a feast of fishes and barley bread and was laid in a manger',[89] and Whitefield condemns the same custom because one would think the children were 'to be initiated into, rather than renounce . . . the pomps . . . of this wicked world'.[90] Thus early introduced to evangelical austerity, the child should continue in that way. 'Never dress them in the fashion. . . . Give them no red shoes, glaring buttons, etc. This fills them with pride, and debases their mind.' In time, it was hoped, the children would grow up and renounce the pleasures of dress of their own accord. One striking example tells how a child did so. Rebuked for wearing ear-rings, she became utterly convinced of the vanity of the world, renounced it, and became a most useful Methodist for more than half a century.[91]

Another snare of the world was dancing. A few Evangelicals countenanced it, but the vast majority condemned it.
Wesley voiced the great objection for them all: 'If dancing be
not evil in itself, yet it leads young women to numberless
evils.'[92] Many echoed Wesley's words. It was the reason for
Whitefield's interference in an apparently harmless New
Year's Day County Dance in America and, if the evangelical
attitude to dancing seems to make much of little, there are
two testimonies from Evangelicals who believed that dancing
had done them great harm when they were children. Hester
Ann Rogers was allowed to dance at eight years old, when
her father died. 'This was a fatal stab to her divine impressions' says her biographer. 'It paved the way to lightness,
trifling, love of pleasure, and various evils.'[93] Adam Clarke's
attack is even more telling, for the words are his own.
'Dancing was to me a preventing influence, an unmixed
moral evil.'[94]

It is difficult to gainsay the children's own objections to
what appears today a relatively harmless pastime, though
there is, perhaps, enough truth in Wesley's condemnation
of it to make its defenders a little uneasy.

Cards were so obviously a device of the devil that few
Evangelicals thought it necessary to warn children against
them. William Goode did list its damnable qualities, however, and these were a 'tendency to excite bad tempers',
an 'almost necessary connexion with playing for money', and
a 'danger of acquiring a taste for it'.[95] Alone among the
Evangelicals, Thomas Adam indulged in cards as a relaxa-
tion for his old age. This ungodly habit is carefully noted
among 'His Defects'. Isaac Milner amused his child niece
Mary with card tricks, but as it was Mary who wrote his
biography this habit is not condemned. The most alarming
proof of the devilish nature of card-playing came to Christopher Hopper. His master, formerly devout, indulged in a
game of cards, sank into a state of melancholy through this
wickedness, and eventually drowned himself.[96] What greater
proof could there be of the hellish nature of cards?

The Evangelicals disagreed about what Christians should and should not read. Berridge, an extremist in all things, incurred Wesley's wrath by banning all reading except the Bible. On a number of occasions school-masters, newly converted, asked advice on whether or not they should teach Classics from heathen authors; might it not corrupt young minds? The general test of suitability of reading was—is it profitable, religiously speaking? Clearly, novels, for instance, were unprofitable. There was usually nothing of God in them, so they were at the least a waste of time, which is God's time, and therefore waste is sin. Worse, they were works of the imagination, and the devil works his wickedness through this medium. It was not long, however, before the Evangelicals enlisted the devil's support in their battle against sin. Hannah More, who had condemned novels in 1799 as 'the most pernicious source of moral corruption', herself published *Coelebs in Search of a Wife* in 1808. Nor could any reasonable person object to her novel, for it is so laboriously moral and correct that the plot is only observed with difficulty. Hannah More had indeed provided material that any Evangelical could read with profit. 'Be careful to read such books only as have a moral or religious tendency', advised the *Evangelical Magazine* in 1800. 'Coelebs' certainly had that.

Just how evil the influence of 'Tales of Love and Maids forsaken' could be on young minds, James Lackington proves. He admits that the Methodists had warned him that to marry a novel-loving girl would lead to his own damnation, and it very nearly did. Years later he looks back over the unregenerate years and wishes he had read nothing but the Bible. 'That precious book enabled me to breakfast, dine and sup on watergruel only . . . with a cheerful countenance and a merry heart.'[97] It is doubtful if the Bible has ever received a more remarkable tribute.

The Evangelicals were virtually unanimous in condemning plays. The only important exception is Hannah More, whose friendship with Garrick and whose facility in producing bad verse tempted her to write two plays, 'Percy' and 'The Fatal Falsehood', the first of which was a remarkable success. She later acknowledged it had been a great mistake, and showed the incompatibility of Tragic Drama with Christianity. She considered that Honour, 'the religion of tragedy', was in opposition to Christianity. Vices in Drama were made great and found 'a dazzling system of worldly morality in direct opposition to the spirit of a religion whose characteristics are charity, meekness, peacableness, long-suffering and gentleness'.[98] She did continue to write sacred dramas for children, but even these were condemned by the Eclectic Society.

Wesley called the current stage a 'sink of all profaneness and debauchery', and many contemporaries, such as Fielding and Swift (neither of an over-tender conscience), agreed with him. This foul condition grew during the period; Wesley had been a lover of good plays in his youth and was passionately fond of Shakespeare. The succeeding Evangelicals all condemned it and warned their children against it. Many tracts were written against the playhouse, and not a few dying saints pleaded with their children from their death-beds to shun Satan there. Arguments against plays vary from the sound to the silly: 'The imitation of thunder and other such works of the Almighty, as in the witch-scene in Macbeth, I think objectionable'.[99] Even Hervey, much less narrow in his views than most Evangelicals, was prepared to take his children to the Theatre, only that they might see the vanity of it, and so want never to return.[100]

The sinfulness of secular music was a particular problem to Evangelicals. All agreed on the wickedness of the 'vulgar and indecent' ballads of the day, which foolish maids were apt to teach children, but it was difficult to condemn all secular music when the co-founder of Methodism had two musical prodigies as his sons, and the founder himself was an occasional concert-goer. Henry Venn found he had unwittingly caused 'great offence' by attending a concert, though he 'never was more serious and devout in my own thoughts' than on that occasion.[101] The general feeling was against secular music, and it was a rash man who dare let his children attend concerts. For the Evangelicals, not only should children's behaviour be blameless, it should also be actively religious. Passivity strongly hinted of wickedness within. 'Stillness' should be accompanied by a Bible or a hymn-book, as an outward sign of inner devoutness.

Games for children were suspect. Any form of play was prohibited at Kingswood, and Charles Wesley, in full agreement with his brother on this point (at least in theory), wrote several hymns for children, equating play with sin. There is something peculiarly horrible in:

> *We for no wordly pleasures plead,*
> *No innocent diversions need,*
> *   As Satan calls his joys:*
> *His rattles let the tempter keep,*
> *Or his own children rock to sleep*
> *   With such amusing toys.*[102]

Usually the Arminians were less harsh than the Calvinists, but this is a striking exception to the general rule. It is ironical that the two sons of the author of such a hymn should become professional performers of 'innocent diversions'.

Rowland Hill allowed games, provided they were innocent. An 'innocent diversion' to him was to walk in the garden, or watch lambs in the fields.

> *Like them, we may cheerfully frolic and play,*
> *If we are as gentle and harmless as they.*[103]

Possibly doubting if hell-bent children were capable of being gentle and harmless, he proceeded to make 'instructive playthings' for them. These he sent for Hannah More's approval. They were 'boxes, covered with coloured paper, and containing, in partitions, the letters of the alphabet, from which improving sentences and texts of Scripture might be found'. All instructions were written in poetry. Verse 3 reads:

> *Thus, kindly instructed, we children may look,*
> *And thankfully read in God's holy Book,*
> *How Jesus, the Saviour, our Lord and our God,*
> *Came down to redeem us by shedding his blood.*

Thoughtful for parents also, Hill's concluding verse instructs children to put away the letters afterwards, or forfeit one penny per missing letter.[104]

Godly conversation was, of course, encouraged, but light or trifling conversation was to be avoided. At all times and in all places children were advised to talk only of the things of God—just how stifling an atmosphere this created is a matter for conjecture, but rules such as 'We have no time given to throw away, but to improve for eternity ... can join in no conversation that is unprofitable',[105] suggest the children must have suffered from severe religious indigestion. Some of them, sounding old before their years to us, shrank from worldly conversation as nervously as their parents. 'I have this day had some friends with me who are quite worldly people: and though our conversation has had, I trust, nothing inconsistent with godliness in it, yet my heart has not been with God. O dreadful state of insensibility!'[106] Much more understandable psychologically is the condition of the little boy who felt deep religious impressions, and 'naturally enough supposed that all who had now heard the same word, would feel as he felt; and after service had concluded, he drew near to some aged professors of religion, and walked by their side, in hopes of hearing from them some religious conversation, that might tend to instruct and benefit his own mind ... but Peter was astonished and grievously disappointed to find those aged and regular attendants on church busily employed in worldly conversation, as careless as though all they had heard of God's long suffering and coming judgement were matters of no account'.[107] The behaviour of their elders must ever have been something of a mystery to devout children.

Mixing with worldly children was forbidden to Evangelicals.

> *But with what playmates e'er you trust*
> *Your darling, O beware!*
> *Example, like corroding rust,*
> *Will tarnish all your care.*[108]

It did not appear to occur to the Evangelicals that failing to understand how the other half lived might be ill preparation for a world their children would eventually have to inhabit without parental oversight. 'Promiscuous Visiting', as the Evangelicals called mixing with those not of their persuasion, was denied to the children, but it was a very dangerous denial.

The denials of the Sabbath were all-embracing. It would be much shorter to list what was allowed rather than what was denied. Unprofitable conversation and visiting were, of course, quite out of the question. The *Evangelical Magazine* thoughtfully suggested a way of dealing with Sabbath intruders. Read the Bible to them. 'You will soon find that those who do not love to hear of Christ, will refrain from calling.'[109] This method was almost certainly efficacious.

All the Evangelicals felt strongly on the subject. The redoubtable Hannah More waged a battle for years over Sabbath Observance. The danger of her crusade was that of mere negativism, and in the popular estimation the evangelical attitude to the Sabbath seemed antique, narrow, and suggestive of a 'holier than thou' outlook on others.

The effect on children must have been depressing. If the paterfamilias, like Francis Newton, was 'so far ... from doing any ordinary work, that he endeavoured not to speak his own words, or to think his own thoughts on that day',[110] then the children must have spent the day longing for Monday morning.

One hymnodist, holding out the bait of play during the

week (the Wesleys would have denied even this) sought to make Sunday sound enjoyable.

> *We must not play on Sunday.*
>   *Because it is a sin;*
> *But we may play on Monday,*
> *On Tuesday, Wednesday, Thursday.*

He also observes, 'We must not laugh on Sunday', but he leads the children to a triumphant conclusion with,

> *Now I love the Sabbath day,*
> *Love it better than my play:*
> *And I very well can spare*
> *This whole day for praise and prayer.*[111]

It is doubtful how many evangelical children really enjoyed the Sabbath Day until their conversion sanctified the whole. Yet more in retrospect approved it and imitated it than abandoned it.

Most of the forementioned denials forced upon evangelical children were denied because they were worldly, sin-infected. A subtler sin, however, remained for those who managed to avoid Satan's more obvious wiles. There was always a danger of 'inordinate affection for things lawful'. Newton's devoted love for his wife was considered a blemish in him; he loved her too much. Charles Wesley wrote some of his most moving poetry on the death of his first-born.

> *Those waving hands no more shall move,*
>   *Those laughing eyes shall smile no more:*
> *He cannot now engage our love*
>   *With sweet insinuating power,*
> *Our weak unguarded hearts ensnare,*
> *And rival his Creator there.*[112]

The child that might have taken God's place in his father's heart was dead. Conversely, children were taught to value God above their parents, above everything in the world. The

teaching was consistent, but it is great credit to the Evangelicals that they were prepared to admit higher authority
over their children even than themselves.

Asceticism was deep in most leading Evangelicals. In the
Wesleys, Whitefield, Henry Venn, Grimshaw, and Adam
Clarke, it took the form of fasts so prolonged that health
was endangered. Cecil deliberately abandoned his two
loves, music and painting. Walker of Truro refused to
marry a woman whom he loved, and who would have made
him an excellent wife, for no apparent reason except that
it would have given him 'temporal happiness'.

This same spirit was inculcated in children. By the
number of denials that were expected of them, by the
published examples of those who had gone before, by
rigorous exclusion of all deeds and thoughts that were not
God-centred, child-Evangelicals were urged to lead ascetic
lives. Before the dawn of Chadbandism, these children led
lives that monks might have considered severe—and the
monks had at least chosen their way of life. When Newton
said of himself, 'I spent the greater part of every day in
reading the Scriptures, in meditation and in prayer. I
fasted often, I even abstained from animal food for three
months. I would hardly answer a question, for fear of
speaking an idle word',[113] he was not only speaking for
himself, but representing the pattern of infant piety for
young Evangelicals. The road to heaven was narrow and
thorny, and there were many side roads to lure the young
away. Only by absolute subjugation of the world in their
hearts could these children press on towards their goal.
Then, and only then, could they approach the one essential
condition of entry.

SALVATION

It was noted earlier that the Evangelicals tended to teach
their children a divided Trinity. As far as the children were
concerned, however, what was bad theologically was sound
psychologically. The child would happily accept a divided

Trinity, since it fitted so admirably into his understanding of his parents. It was easy to understand the variable nature of God through the variable nature of a human father. Just as an earthly father appeared omniscient, omnipresent and omnipotent, was both judge and executioner in matters of law, and frequently seemed disproportionate in punishment, so was God the Father; and just as, once the will was completely given up to him, did an earthly father appear gentle and loving, so was God the Son: and just as—to carry an unhappy comparison to its conclusion—the presence of an earthly father was felt even in his absence, so was God the Holy Spirit. In child-terms, the Evangelical idea of God was perfectly comprehensible.

The only exceptions to the necessity of Conversion—the normal manner of Salvation—were infants who died too soon to be born a second time. This problem caused the Evangelicals much thought, for their whole theology was based on the idea of a second birth. They did grant the exceptions, however, usually on the ground of baptismal grace still applying.

The first step towards Conversion of infants not excepted by grace was penitence. It was the custom with most Evangelicals to pray with children and remind them of their sins. Without a due sense of sorrow for their wickedness children could not be saved. We read in Rowland Hill's *Lives and Deaths of Good Children* of 'a child monstrously wicked' who committed 'vile practices' in early infancy, and later 'begged to be washed in the blood of Christ'. Another child 'would weep over her sinful state, and frequently would retire into her chamber, and there privately cry against her sins'. A sense of sin was expected very early in Evangelical children. 'Naughtiness', 'Mischief', and 'Fibs' were unknown; 'Wickedness', 'Depravity', and 'Damnable Lies' were rife. Special prayers were written for children, to assist them in their penitence. 'A Prayer that a child may say before the Lord at any time, but especially when his Heart is broken for sin', begins: 'Pardon me that though so young, I have been so vile a sinner in thy sight. Give me a weeping eye, and a broken heart, for all my transgressions.'[114] Penitential hymns were written, and the Law with all its implications was as regularly the beginning of sermons for children as the Gospel was the end.

Conversion was not unknown in very early infancy. Indeed, some Evangelicals expected it. Grimshaw noted that 'the Holy Ghost begins with us in our infancy', but realized that this did not of necessity mean more than 'awful and heart-affecting thoughts about a God, and judgement, death, and eternity'.[115] Wesley, however, quotes very early examples. One girl at two and a half, and a boy at four, only showed great seriousness, but another child, a girl of four, Wesley buried 'in the full assurance of faith'. Two other girls, one eight, one less, were as soundly converted, one 'dying as an hundred years old', the other 'as serious as one of forty'.[116] Wesley also found proofs of very young conversions in his Weardale Society. There were 165 members in all, of whom 43 were children. Thirty of these 'are rejoicing in the love of God'. For special mention Wesley picked out girls of $8\frac{1}{2}$ 'as serious as a woman of 50' (this seems a strange test today); $9\frac{1}{2}$, 'of uncommon understanding'; 10, 'full of faith and love'; and 14, 'as a mother among them.'[117] The solitary boy, a 10-year old, was as 'wise and stayed as a man'.

It is difficult from this sort of comment to escape the suspicion that Wesley tended to value precocity over much. His test seems to be 'seriousness'. Very 'serious' in childhood himself, he considered he was ripe for conversion at ten. Yet in the chronicles of hagiology, child saints more commonly retain child likeness: their maturity is spiritual, not social. The terminology of Wesley's praise, however, is uncertain. 'Serious' may contain other elements besides spiritual concern, sobriety, and a long list of negative attributes. Certainly other Evangelicals quote conversions at very early periods. Charles Wesley wrote a number of hymns expecting Salvation in childhood; others accepted them, as the Wesleys did, only if the fruits of conversion were present, or death intervened.

Adolescence was a common time for conversion, possibly the commonest. Detailed accounts show the variety of religious experience even under similar conditions. The essence of each account is the complete surrender of the will to Christ, just as all the preliminary stages are the battles of self-will against His absolute demand. Unfortunately, too many accounts of conversion are written in Canaanitish phrases which make them sound stilted or even insincere. One author says of his experience at thirteen: 'Convictions being reared, pectoral guiltiness coagitated my soul'.[118] That many sounding so were very far from being so, the later lives prove. The sheer difficulty of describing a spiritual experience except in the terms of the education which led up to it is the problem. Saturated in biblical phrase and evangelical cliché through their formative years, the children could hardly be expected to explain the inexplicable in more lucid terms.

That some 'conversions' were false, or at any rate did not last, all the Evangelicals well knew. Lackington's case is interesting as he is able to give a sneering, unsympathetic account of his own 'conversion' from the viewpoint of his later hatred of it, and finally retract almost all he says before his death. It is interesting also in that it reveals the successive changes that led to his conversion. He first tells how his brother George had a spiritual experience. 'By this sermon the fallow ground of poor George's heart was ploughed up; he was now persuaded that the innocent and good life he had led would only sink him deeper into hell'. George knew 'he was in a state of damnation'. George then began to proselytize. He 'very kindly gave us to understand, that he was sure we were in a very deplorable state, without hope, and without God in the world, being under the curse of the Law'. This was orthodox evangelical teaching and George was an orthodox young convert. Then it was James's turn. He was terrified by a sermon which assured him he would be 'damn'd, and double damn'd, and treble damn'd, and damn'd for ever'. 'At last', he continues, 'I got my imagination to the proper pitch, and thus was I born again in an instant' and 'became a great favourite of heaven.'[119] The sneering tone does not succeed in denying that the experience, though it had not lasting power, was very real at the time, nor does Lackington deny that the loss of his spiritual experience followed his failure to live up to his own principles. Religious 'doubts' often follow moral failure. His attack on Methodism in general, and their ways of conversion in particular, hint of the anger of a man who resents others attaining what he could not reach. 'They work on the fears of the most virtuous; youth and innocence fall victims daily before their threats of hell and damnation ... often by them sunk into an irrecoverable state of gloomy despondence and horrible despair.' These victims are 'hocus-pocusly converted'. Lackington considers himself as one 'who, from a gay, volatile, dissipated young fellow, was at once metamorphosed into a dull, moping, praying, psalm-singing fanatic, continually reprehending all about me for their harmless mirth and gaiety'.[120]

So Lackington wrote long afterwards, but his experience was neither as imaginary nor ephemeral as he thought. Like many other converts, he became a 'backslider', and also like many others, he returned to the fold before it was too late. Theologically, Calvinists and Arminians differed over Conversion, and it was over the question of backsliders that the difference became apparent. For Calvinists, Conversion was the conviction that they were inevitably sealed for heaven; backsliding was strongly indicative of preordained damnation. For Arminians, Conversion was a consciousness of Christ having died for their sins, and the sinners being accepted by Him, but the sinners could reject Christ's offer.

> *Ah, Lord, with trembling, I confess*
> *A gracious soul may fall from grace.*

For children this distinction could have meant little, except that Arminian teaching probably kept a foot in the door of hope long after Calvinists considered it shut and bolted.

The Evangelicals differed also over the speed of conversion. Wesley, quoting apostolic authority, believed it was instantaneous. He later modified his views slightly, but not as far as his preaching was concerned. Later Evangelicals, however, were not so sure, and considered that a gradual conversion was possible. 'The way of the Lord is various with different persons', writes an anonymous author of a Memoir.[121] 'Some are brought instantly out of darkness into marvellous light; their convictions are sudden, deep, and short: in others, the way of the Lord is prepared as the morning, with a gradual, and almost imperceptibly increasing light.' Another writer suggests that sudden conversion was normal in those 'who have lived in the contempt or neglect of religion';[122] others could not expect such a sudden change. The very title of a later pamphlet, *Anecdotes of Remarkable Conversions* (1815), suggests that the thirty sudden conversions which are given were unusual in their suddenness by that period. The later the date, in fact, the more rare do sudden conversions become, and the less violent is the travail of this second birth. The change is the result of evangelical teaching. In the early period of the Revival, the message was new to the hearers. Salvation by faith alone, the worthlessness of works, hell without a second birth, total depravity—all these things had a shocking freshness which could startle or terrify children into violent change. In time the freshness was lost; the message no longer shocked; the majority of children heard the same warnings from their earliest years and grew accustomed to them. Conversion then became a gradual absorption of their parents' ideas into their own minds; little by little lip-service became heart-service, and the second birth was achieved almost imperceptibly.

In the same way did the convulsions, so common at the beginning of the Revival, become more and more rare as the century drew to a close. What had been thought an almost inevitable accompaniment of conversion was later seen to be merely an accidental accompaniment, one sympton of violent change when the evangelical message was new. The later history of the children converted at the great Revival at Everton, when for several days together fits, trances, screams, and faintings accompanied the preaching, is unknown. It is certain that later Evangelicals regarded convulsions with disapproval. Too much ridicule had been attached to their party because of them. Even the early Evangelicals had been most unhappy about them. Those chiefly involved were the two Wesleys, Whitefield, and Berridge. Of these Charles Wesley did all in his power to prevent them; Whitefield disapproved of them and only reluctantly accepted them as an unfortunate necessity; John Wesley was shocked by them, investigated them carefully and then had to accept them as genuine; and Berridge alone appears to have delighted in them.

However much the trappings of conversion altered, children were still taught that it was the one essential of life and the passport to heaven. Nothing else mattered. All life and all future happiness consisted in the absolute surrender of oneself to God.

REFERENCES

1. G. W. E. Russell, *The Household of Faith*, pp. 239–40.
2. R. A. Knox, *Enthusiasm*, p. 545.
3. *Poetical Works*, IV, p. 260.
4. Ibid. VI, p. 402.
5. R. S. Hardy, *Life of Grimshaw*, p. 41.
6. *Poetical Works*, VI, p. 394.
7. *An Account of the Religious and Literary Life of the Rev. Adam Clarke*, ed. J. B. B. Clarke, I, p. 58.
8. Rowland Hill, *Hymns*.
9. Mrs Edwina Gray, *Papers and Diaries of a York Family*, pp. 81–2.
10. L. F. Church, *Early Methodist People*, p. 243.
11. *Poetical Works*, VII, p. 99.
12. *Arminian Magazine* (1781), p. 535.
13. Rowland Hill, 'Lives and Deaths of Good Children', from *Instructions for Children*.
14. Three Old Boys, *History of Kingswood School*, p. 48.

15. Thos Jackson, *The Lives of Early Methodist Preachers*, IV, pp. 228–9.
16. *An account of the Religious and Literary Life of the Rev. Adam Clarke*, ed. J. B. B. Clarke, I, pp. 68–9.
17. L. Tyerman, *The Life of George Whitefield*, II, p. 330.
18. R. S. Hardy, *Life of Grimshaw*, p. 63.
19. *An account of the Life, and dealings of God with Silas Told*, by himself, p. 9.
20. *Poetical Works*, VIII, p. 422.
21. Ibid. VI, p. 459.
22. *Arminian Magazine* (1782), pp. 468–72.
23. Rowland Hill, *Lives and Deaths of Good Children*, Example III.
24. *Poetical Works*, V, pp. 84–5.
25. Ibid.
26. Rowland Hill, *Lives and Deaths of Good Children*, Example III.
27. Ibid. Example V.
28. Ibid. Example XI.
29. Ibid. Examples VII, IV.
30. Rowland Hill, 'Hell', *Hymns*.
31. *Poetical Works*, VI, p. 429.
32. *Arminian Magazine* (1780), p. 25.
33. *Memoirs of the Life of the Rev. Peard Dickinson*, ed. Joseph Pearson, p. 14.
34. Rowland Hill, *Instructions for Children*.
35. Isaac Watts, Hymn, 'Praise to God'.
36. 'For a Sick Child', *Poetical Works*, VII, p. 82.
37. L. Tyerman, *Wesley's Designated Successor*, p. 260.
38. *Poetical Works*, VI, p. 411.
39. Ibid. VI, p. 426.
40. Ibid. VI, p. 396, 'For an Unconverted Child'.
41. Rowland Hill, *Hymns*, 'A Child's Confession to be said when sorry for a sin newly committed'.
42. Wm Jay, 'Memoirs of the Rev. John Clarke', *Works*, VIII, p. 446.
43. J. A. Hanway, *A Comprehensive View of Sunday Schools*, p. 72.
44. J. Jackson, *A Short account of Miss Anna Wrangham* (1805).
45. *Works*, II, pp. 477–8.
46. L. F. Church, *Early Methodist People*, p. 245.
47. *Poetical Works*, VI, pp. 426–7.
48. Watts, *Hymns*, 'Solemn Thoughts of God and Death'.
49. J. W. Middleton, *An Ecclesiastical Memoir of the first four decades of the reign of George III*, pp. 98–9.
50. L. Tyerman, *Wesley's Designated Successor*, p. 5.
51. L. F. Church, *Early Methodist People*, p. 245.
52. Thos Scott, *The Force of Truth*, p. 4.
53. J. Newton, *Life of Grimshaw*, p. 42.
54. R. S. Hardy, *Life of Grimshaw*, p. 16.
55. *Lives of Early Methodist Preachers*, ed. Thomas Jackson.
56. *An account of the Religious and Literary Life of the Rev. Adam Clarke*, ed. J. B. B. Clarke, pp. 26–7.
57. *Works*, II, pp. 498–9.

58. Hervey, *Works*, p. 27.
59. Rev. Mr M——, 'A Soliloquy', *Evangelical Magazine* (1780), p. 562.
60. Wm. Jay, *Works*, V, p. 7.
61. *Poetical Works*, V, p. 227.
62. *Life of Henry Longden of Sheffield*, by himself, pp. 41–6.
63. Thos Wood, *The Season of youth favoured with the Divine Presence* (1814), p. 5.
64. J. A. Hanway, *A Comprehensive View of Sunday Schools*, p. 67.
65. Walker of Truro, *Fifty-two Sermons*, p. LXXXI.
66. Wm. Jay, *Works*, V, p. 177.
67. *Life of Henry Longden of Sheffield*, by himself, p. 22.
68. L. Tyerman, *Life of the Rev. George Whitefield*, II, p. 556.
69. M. G. Jones, Quoted in *Hannah More*, p. 163.
70. *Poetical Works*, VI, p. 406.
71. J. Venn, *Annals of a Clerical Family*, p. 104.
72. *Evangelical Magazine* (1794), pp. 253–4.
73. Ibid. (1797), pp. 258–9.
74. *Works*, II, p. 261.
75. T. Bingham, *An account of the Life and Death of Elizabeth Radder of Whitchurch, Hants* (1815).
76. *Poetical Works*, II, p. 183.
77. Ibid. VI, p. 395.
78. Rev. Thos Adam, *An exposition of the Four Gospels*, ed. Westoby, p. 123.
79. *Poetical Works*, VII, p. 139.
80. John Pearson, *Life of William Hey, Esq., F.R.S.*, Part II, p. 47.
81. Mrs Gaskell, *Life of Charlotte Brontë*, p. 44.
82. *Poetical Works*, VII, p. 179.
83. Mary Milner, *Life of Isaac Milner*, pp. 419–20.
84. *Evangelical Magazine* (1799), p. 354.
85. L. Tyerman, *Life of the Rev. George Whitefield*, I, p. 36.
86. T. T. Bidulph, *The Inconsistency of Conformity to this world* (1803).
87. W. H. Proby, *Annals of the Low Church Party*, I, p. 256.
88. John Bowles, *Remarks on Modern Female Manners* (1802).
89. Hannah More *On Baptism*, Cheap Repository Tract (possibly written by Zachary Macaulay).
90. L. Tyerman, *Life of the Rev. George Whitefield*, I, p. 419.
91. G. J. Stevenson, *City Road Chapel*, p. 173.
92. J. Wesley, Letter to Miss Bishop, *Works*, XIII, p. 39.
93. Rev. Thos Coke, *A Funeral Sermon ... Mrs Hester Ann Rogers*, p. 15.
94. *An account of the Religious and Literary Life of the Rev. Adam Clarke*, ed. J. B. B. Clarke, I, p. 66.
95. W. Goode, *A Memoir of the late Rev. Wm Goode*, p. 95.
96. *Arminian Magazine* (1781), p. 25.
97. *The Confessions of J. Lackington, by himself*, Part I, p. 2–6.
98. M. G. Jones, *Hannah More*, p. 39.
99. J. H. Pratt, *Eclectic Notes*, p. 161.
100. J. Hervey, *Works*, p. 528.

101. J. Venn, *Annals of a Clerical Family*, p. 107.
102. *Poetical Works*, VI, p. 439.
103. Rowland Hill, 'A Sonnet of Instruction'.
104. E. Sidney, *Life of the Rev. Rowland Hill*, pp. 400–3.
105. L. F. Church, *Early Methodist People*, p. 223.
106. *Christian Observer* (1802), p. 757.
107. Joseph Barker, *Memoir of Peter Shaw* (1839).
108. Wm. Jay, *Works*, VIII, p. 447.
109. *Evangelical Magazine* (1798), p. 495.
110. Rev. Dr Robert Newton, *Memoirs of the late Mr Francis Newton of Thorpe*, p. 15.
111. Author unknown; quoted in W. H. Proby, *Annals of the Low Church Party*, I, p. 255.
112. *Poetical Works*, VI, p. 253.
113. Sir James Stephen, quoted in *Essays in Ecclesiastical Biography*, II, p. 65.
114. Rowland Hill, *Prayers for Children*.
115. R. S. Hardy, *Life of Grimshaw*, p. 4.
116. *Works*, II, pp. 325–6, 191; I, p. 472; II, p. 10 respectively.
117. Ibid. XIII, p. 339.
118. Rev. John Gibbons, *The Mourning Saint Among the Willows* (1788), Ch. VI, p. 20.
119. *Memoirs of James Lackington, Bookseller*, by himself, pp. 79, 85.
120. Ibid. pp. 94–5, 156.
121. *A brief account of the Life and Death of Barbara Walker*, No date, Author unknown (c. 1800).
122. *Christian Observer* (1802), p. 756.

CHAPTER VI

The Fruit of their Teaching

THE PATTERN OF PIETY

IT HAS ALREADY been suggested that the ideal evangelical pattern of piety was the retention of baptismal innocence until death. This possibility was so remote that it would have been ignored had not Wesley promulgated it as a theory. Although, furthermore, all Evangelicals conducted their children's religious upbringing with this implicit hope, the ideal was never realized, nor was it expected. Wesley's theory remains unproven, and no evangelical household claimed it for children except—and only tacitly then—when a child died in very early infancy.

The very rootedness of sin in human nature all but excluded the possibility, and thus it was that Evangelicals always preached the necessity of a second birth, and watched for signs of it in their children. A little of the devil, it seemed, was our human inheritance, no matter what safeguards were taken, but righteousness should be followed as early as possible. 'There is', said Sir James Stephen, 'a natural history of religious conversions. It commences with melancholy, advances through contrition to faith, is then conducted to tranquillity, and after a while, to rapture, and subsides at length into an abiding consolation and peace'.[1] This was the pattern of piety which the Evangelicals expected.

They were not disappointed. Obviously the processes of conversion are much more likely to happen in a Communion that expects them. But this does not explain all. Evangelical piety was not proven in an hour or a day or a week. Children might well, under strong parental pressure

and the force of brief emotional stress, feel guilt, or melancholy, or rapture for a while, under an imagined 'conversion'. But unless it lasted, its falsity was soon obvious.
Children were not to give up the pleasant things of life—
music, dancing, reading romances, gay clothes, etc.—for a
while, but for ever. They were to embrace lives of religious
austerity, which their own chosen companions would be
watching carefully, ready to denounce them should they
falter. No merely artificial stimulus could persuade children .
to this. Evangelical religious education survived infancy
and carried most of its children into adulthood. Long after
the parents were dust their prescribed pattern lived on to
mould the next generation.

Of course, there were failures. There had always been
failures. Wesley had often been perplexed at the sudden
unaccountable losses among his people. Sometimes the
fault lay with the parents: 'It must be allowed ... that the
bad courses which some religiously educated children have
taken, are to be accounted for ... from the want of corres-
pondency between the profession and the life—the prayers
and the practice of the parent'.[2] The father who sang,

A saint indeed I long to be,
And lead my faithful family
In the celestial road,[3]

but whose practice fell short of the ideal must have been
common. And even the most saintly parent might die and
leave children like ten-year-old William Gray who 'lost his relish for religion, having no longer his mother's watchful care'.[4]

The chief cause of loss, however, was the failure of the
children themselves. As far as Arminians were concerned,
the will was absolutely free to choose good or evil, and the
bias of nature runs towards evil. As for Calvinists, the
doctrine of predestination inevitably meant that some must
be damned. If apparent Irresistible Grace had somehow
been resisted, then there was a strong presumption that the
lambs were really kids, and the sheep must be goats.

The Evangelical father longed for maturity in his children, that the infantile lack of seriousness might be banished.

> *When, dear Lord, ah! tell us when*
> *Shall we be in knowledge men?*[5]

Infinite trouble was taken with the children, and yet:

> *After all our teachers' pains,*
> *Little good in us remains.*[6]

Always, it seemed, children wanted to be childish:

> *Suddenly our goodness fails,*
> *Levity again prevails.*[7]

In another context Gladstone writes: 'There is causation by parentage and there is also causation by the way of opposition and reaction.'[8] He was writing of the connexion between the Evangelicals and the Tractarians, but the point applies equally to the reaction of some children to evangelical training. In Samuel Butler's *The Way of All Flesh* and Edmund Gosse's *Father and Son* are two striking instances of reaction against the religious influence of parents. Certainly some losses could be explained this way.

Yet if there were losses, there were successes too. The 'sampling technique' has its dangers. One can never get enough 'samples' to be confident of a conclusion. Nor is any particular 'sample' ever sufficiently full to be completely comprehensible. Since, however, no other method can test the efficiency of evangelical religious education, it must be employed here.

But first one fully documented account of religious progress will be considered. Mary Gilbert, who lived from 1751 to 1768, kept a journal of her spiritual life. Wesley edited and published it with his fullest approbation, calling it 'a masterpiece in its kind'; and its young author 'a prodigy of a child! Soon ripe, and soon gone'.[9] It is Wesley's approval that makes this case so important. The *Journal* was the finest documentary proof of the pattern of child piety that he knew; it was an ideal of its type.

The *Journal* begins when the child is fourteen. All her thoughts are God-centred, and she notes any falling-off from seriousness. 'I found a blessing while dressing, but lost it by giving way to levity.' Such self-reproaches are scattered throughout. She quotes a number of sermons, the texts typically evangelical, and she copies out portions of Charles Wesley's hymns. The visits of John Wesley are important days for her. She dreams of conversion, but in spite of 'strict self-examination' she is still tortured by her inability to live up to her ideal.

Later the same year she goes on the inevitable corpse-visiting. 'In the afternoon we went to Mr C———r, to see the corpse of her [*sic*] daughter. I was not at all shocked,' she writes, but she had 'serious reflections. ... So, just so, thought I, must I shortly be: I must die, be stretched in a coffin, and laid in the silent grave. ...' After this date the death-wish begins to grip her. Early in 1766 she is 'in great affliction for the loss of poor, or rather happy, little Ned H———. ... O that I was as safely landed on the happy shore'. A little later she is 'oppressed all this day with that tormenting passion, the fear of death, insomuch that I had not comfort in any thing'.

Continually close to conversion, Mary Gilbert always finds it eludes her grasp. 'When shall I find free access to the throne, and be enabled to call Jesus mine, my Lord and my God?' she writes, and occasionally her pleas become cries for help: 'Lord, save, or I perish.'

Soon after being a bearer with four other girls at a funeral, Mary Gilbert senses that her own end is not far away, and rests her confidence of heaven in an early death—the hope presumably being that God would not make such heavy demands of one so young; 'I was confined to my bed, being much indisposed. O what a short transition from time to eternity! I thought much of dying, but felt no fear: not because I was ready, but I firmly believed the Lord would cut short his work in righteousness if he called me.'

So it was. Though on her death-bed Mary Gilbert was deaf and dumb through 'putrid fever' (which 'rendered her situation very trying, as well as deprived her friends of that profit and satisfaction, which might otherwise have been expected'). Wesley's comments leave no doubt that she was converted in the hour of her death—'Soon ripe, and soon gone'.

This, then, was the pattern of piety; struggling by one's own righteousness to God, inevitably failing, and so flinging oneself on Him in the act of conversion.

THE FRUIT

The first case for consideration is a dismal failure. The tenth Earl of Huntingdon, son of the Countess, became notorious for his 'infidel principles and long determined hostility to evangelical religion'.[10] It is only fair to add that the boy was introduced into 'the polite world' by Lord Chesterfield, who looked upon him as 'my adopted son'.[11] Few boys could withstand an influence as pernicious as his Lordship's; both his son and his 'adopted son' became wastrels.

The two sons of Charles Wesley, already mentioned, were almost equally unfortunate examples of evangelical training. Charles was 'incapable of excelling in anything but music',[12] and Samuel made a brief excursion to Rome. Neither ever showed serious religious inclinations.

Benjamin Ingham's son was 'disappointing'. He is briefly mentioned as preaching for a while among Wesley's Societies, but fades into obscurity after that.

Those, it seems, were total failures. Another small group cannot be counted as failures, since they were converted at the eleventh hour, after disgraceful lives. The Evangelicals would reasonably have rejoiced in them since, notwithstanding their evil ways, they finally attained heaven; and that, ultimately, was all that mattered. 'An education conducted judicially on Christian principles seldom fails, through the divine blessing, of ultimate success, *however long the desired end may be delayed.*'[13]

Such a case was Henry Perronet, whom Wesley buried. He 'had been a child of sorrow from his infancy',[14] but he died well. So did Grimshaw's drunkard son, John, whose dying words were: 'What will my father say, when he sees that I am got to heaven?'[15] The fullest account of such a case is that of Basil Owen Woodd, son of Basil Woodd. The boy was brought up under his father's roof to protect him from the world, but at ten years old an acquaintance introduced him, and through sheer weakness of character he grew up a profligate. There appears to have been no vice in him, but a total lack of will-power. He was continually in debt, a theatre-goer and a brothel-haunter. Of himself he said: 'My errors are ... owing to want of resolution, rather than to wrong intention.'[16] Finally a severe illness attacked him, and he was grateful for the time it afforded for repentance. He borrowed Herbert's words as he lay dying: 'I am sorry I have nothing to present to my merciful God but sin and misery: but the first is pardoned, and a few hours will now put a period to the latter.'[17] The whole moving account the father published for the benefit of children.

The largest number of cases considered showed infant piety, followed by a period of worldliness, varying in length from a month or two to several years, and a conversion leading to a mature life of a deeply religious nature. It would appear that the evangelical influence tended to wear off about the time of adolescence, and that the return to the fold was commonly in the late 'teens. Catherine Corbett was a typical case of this type. 'Before I was ten years old ... I spent many hours in secret, weeping, and praying to the Lord, to take me to himself.' (This is strikingly like Mary Gilbert.) 'I was so much afraid of pride that I could hardly be persuaded to put on any new clothes, lest they should make me think better of myself; and I had a continual fear of dying or saying any thing to offend God: so that my relations often used to say, "The child is not for this world".'

This stage, however, passed, as it so frequently did. 'Between 14 and 15, I began to keep company with girls of my own age. By this means, I soon grew like them; I was less and less serious, till all the good impressions I had once, were entirely vanished away.'[18] But they were not entirely vanished, for Catherine Corbett recovered her lost piety and died sure of heaven.

This case could be paralleled dozens of times. Indeed, it is so common that—albeit the 'sampling' technique is imperfect—it must be considered the usual pattern.

A third group remains. Data for this group are so slight that many of the cases may belong to the category already considered; it is impossible to say. This group consists of children who were brought up under evangelical influence and remained true to it throughout their lives without any *known* period of straying from the fold. Some of these cases almost become genealogical tables, successive generations following evangelically on. John Venn's amazing claim that he was 'a clergyman, and the son of one, according to tradition, for thirteen generations' (the last one, many generations later, died as Master of Queens' College, Cambridge, only a few years ago) is not entirely relevant as many of his clerical ancestors lived before the Revival, but lists almost as impressive are found both among families of the Establishment and of Methodism.

What of the situation today? Little of this study is of use if it cannot be related to present needs.

Today the viewpoint is less rigorous. This was already so by the turn of the nineteenth century. 'Their sons', said Sir James Stephen of the second generation, 'adopted the same creed with equal sincerity and undiminished earnestness, but with a far keener sense of the hindrances opposed to the indiscriminate and rude exhibition of it.'[19] The impression given at this date is that the cause mellowed and—an implicit assumption—was therefore a finer one.

It is extremely doubtful if anyone would claim that the cause today is only a riper form of the old one; still more doubtful if anyone would consider the cause finer because many of those brought up under evangelical influence today tend to be apologetic about it, as if seriousness in matters of religion were slightly embarrassing. They are anxious, far from boasting of their difference, to plead their unity with other religious thought. They are, indeed, what their eighteenth-century counterparts would have called latitudinarians.

This is not, of course, universally true, but it is a tendency which has become more and more marked with passing time. In part it is the inevitable decline of a great religious movement. Every revival in history has been followed by its decline until the dying embers were rekindled; it may well be that we are due for a revival now. In part evangelicalism is affected by the disease of the age, apathy. And it is also true that it is in times of hardship and among the most unprivileged that the spirit of Evangelicalism is most likely to flourish. Today there is little hardship and there are few unprivileged, at least as far as social welfare is concerned. Evangelically speaking, the times are out of joint.

Very few evangelicals today practise the creed as their forefathers taught it. The very phrase 'a far keener sense of the hindrances opposed to the indiscriminate and rude exhibition of it', quoted above, suggests how even fifty years ago the essence of Evangelicalism had been diluted. The 'exhibition' of their faith was of paramount importance to the originators. 'Indiscriminate' and 'rude', as far as religion was concerned, were adjectives without meaning. To men who believed and taught that religion was the sole occupation of life, and that the first duty of a believer was to proselytize, Sir James Stephen's praise was damnable criticism. The evangelical stresses listed in Chapter 1, seen in the light of Evangelicalism today, afford interesting comparisons.

In theory, evangelical theology has not altered radically, though High Calvinism is now rare. Yet the very starting-point of their theology, Original Sin, has a lesser place in their system, and many frankly doubt the theory.

If present-day Evangelicals still believe that nothing except religion matters, their actions seem often to deny it. They do not, as they did, keep themselves to themselves, and in their gregariousness they have lost their exclusiveness. They are still propagandists of their faith, but are much less militant than formerly. They fear the stigma of vulgarity more than they love the duty of religious propaganda. Fear of the world is almost vanished. Modern Evangelicals have—naturally—found the world a pleasanter place than their forebears; rather than reject it they have come to terms with it. The Doctrine of Personal Salvation is still central in their thought, but many—most, perhaps—would admit what few of their ancestors would admit, that God can work in man's heart in many ways, and the process of regeneration might be very slow, slow to the point of imperceptibility. So also is the weak hold on Church order less obvious when each denomination has its own meeting-place, fully authorized, its own ministers, and its own order of service. It is curious how so many cling tenaciously to their own peculiar ways, when their ancestors cared nothing for order, knowing it to be inessential. Social Christianity the Evangelicals have modified, offering assistance in new directions as the State has progressively taken over their charities.

The methods of teaching have also undergone considerable alteration. Catechizing is now rare. A few hymns are still sung (only two by Charles Wesley), but the 'hell-fire' element has been deleted. Further, those hymns for children which remain are not as typically Evangelical as those no longer sung. Modern prayers are a vast improvement on the earlier ones; they show a much greater understanding of children's minds. It is also as well, perhaps, that the Evangelicals of today write comparatively few books for children. The mawkish Sunday-school prize books of the last century are now less common. Nearly all were badly written. For some inexplicable reason it seems impossible to write a good children's story of evangelical flavour without sentimentality, moral bludgeoning, and pious clichés.

For the rest: tracts specifically for children are rare; pictures are too universal a method of appeal to be analysed as 'Evangelical' or 'non-Evangelical'; magazines though less important and less theological can still be bought, and they often contain child doggerel which passes for poetry; Sunday-schools still produce plays with evangelical tendencies for children, but they are commonly of poor quality, containing the general faults of such children's books; journals and diaries, alone of the methods, are obsolete.

The three great media of teaching have lost much of their power, especially the home. Family worship, the most important educational medium of the Revival, is no longer common. I have the strongest reasons for supposing it rare. School influence is largely represented by Sunday-schools. Kingswood alone survives from the earliest period and here, under the recent leadership of a great headmaster, the tradition is liberal. His system (and a remarkably effective one) was to inculcate through the Chapel and the atmosphere of the School an evangelical spirit which the boys were free to ignore—but didn't. The normal pattern of religious development at Kingswood was the one quoted above as normal even under the sternest influence: early piety, doubts during early teenage years, final acceptance of the evangelical tenets. The Church remains central in a young evangelical life, preaching is still the acceptable means of conversion, and only among one element of modern Evangelicals is there a consciousness that the priestly element of the ministry has a significance.

The most serious loss in modern Evangelicalism is that of home influence. If many changes in evangelical education have been necessary—and I believe they have—it is most certain that the loss of religion in the home can only be deplored. Only a return to this first medium can prevent the former strength of evangelical witness being weakened, becoming unsure of itself, apologetic rather than dynamic, historical pride replacing contemporary greatness. A return to the exact pattern of the first Evangelicals would be as unwise as it would be impracticable, but a failure to use home as the cradle of religion would be suicidal.

It remains to consider the merits and the failings of the evangelical system of education. The failings, since they are commonly supposed to be the whole story, will be considered first.

The most obvious fault of the Evangelicals—yet a fault they considered the chief virtue of their system—was the cloistering process by which children were kept from the world. As they should have realized, such a system inevitably left children unprepared for the world when they had to meet it, and it was usually at the most difficult time of adolescence that the shock came. Further, the system could not really be enforced (as Basil Woodd's experience proves), and the little knowledge of the world that infant prisoners managed to learn might well prove a dangerous thing. This charge could be brought against few Evangelicals today; perhaps it is better so.

A second charge levelled against the Evangelicals is that of severity. If this is taken to mean mental severity, then the charge is fair. Repressive their system certainly was. Yet the Evangelicals are often accused of harshness in their dealings with children, and this is rather different. Most of them loved children and would have been deeply hurt at the imputation. Of the great leaders, Whitefield alone appears to have been harsh (Cornelius Winter's opinion and two strange incidents on board ship suggest it)[20] and not harsh even then by eighteenth-century standards. The rest constantly preached and practised mildness, notwithstanding the essential severity of their creed. So do they today.

Enforcing precocity in children is an evangelical fault more difficult to deny. From birth evangelical parents expected a maturity in their children both social and spiritual. 'Except ye be converted and become as grown people, ye shall in no wise enter the kingdom of heaven'[21] may be an exaggeration of the truth, but not a gross one.

Yet the age encouraged precocity; the Evangelicals had no prerogative of it. In 1804 Macaulay, then four years old, answered an enquiry about some hot coffee spilt over him with 'Thank you, Madam, the agony is abated'.[22] He spoke as a child of the age, not as an Evangelical.

The Evangelicals did, however, tend to force a religious precocity. Joseph Pearson as a small boy listened to 149 sermons in one year, and Jane Treffry 'read the greater part of the Bible before she was four years old'.[23] The emotions of children were deliberately worked upon in religious meetings in order to produce a sense of sin and so conversion.

The most curious aspect of this fault is that the Evangelicals seemed aware of the danger. Wesley, defending himself against the charge of giving too religious an education, ingenuously writes *A Thought on the Manner of Educating Children* as if his system could not possibly be attacked on that head. Cecil, in *Family Worship*, observes that 'The old Dissenters wearied their families', and urges evangelical parents to avoid the pitfall. Yet at the same time we find Thomas Walsh, deeply influenced by Wesley, nearly killing himself through refusing to sleep on the grounds, 'Should a man rob God?';[24] we find Mrs Sherwood offering her children a sermon in place of a fun-fair; and we find that it is a common practice to badger children continually about the state of their souls, and await conversion often with ill-concealed impatience. Certain it is, however, that religious precocity is no longer a failing. Yet—alarming thought!—have the Evangelicals thrown away the baby with the bath water?

Another common charge levelled against the Evangelicals was that of spiritual pride: it was often stated that it was inculcated in children. It is true that the attitude;—

> *Hither by special mercy led,*
> *A little flock, a chosen seed,*
> *We shun the paths of men*—[25]

might encourage pride in weaker vessels, but in general the

tremendous emphasis on original sin, and the safeguards to ensure the godliness of the converted (e.g. Society Meetings) must have made spiritual pride rare in children. True it is that pious children often wept for the sins of others; but tears for their own sins flowed even more copiously. All religious systems have their own peculiar dangers: if that of Evangelicalism was spiritual pride, then as far as children were concerned it almost always remained as a danger only. Today spiritual pride must be rare indeed—and so are saints.

Their abuse of the weapon of fear is the last alleged fault of the evangelical system. The Evangelicals would have attempted to justify their use of it. 'Which is better? To go unafraid to hell, or through fear to attain heaven?' It becomes uncomfortably difficult to answer. Modern theory abhors the use of fear in education. Yet fear still is the only universal deterrent from crime. Evangelical theory might also have defended itself here on the grounds that fear for the young is a suitable goad at least for 'mere morality', for not until maturity dawns does the pure love of God appear sufficient. Again it is difficult to deny it. Certain it is that the chief weapon in the evangelical armoury for the young was fear of hell; how justified they were must remain an open question.

Many of the merits of evangelical religious education were later unacknowledged because other branches of the Church borrowed them and forgot the debt. With some exceptions (it would be a great injustice to High Churchmen to suggest that their cause was unrepresented for two decades) the people who treated religion seriously from 1730 to 1750 were the Evangelicals. It was their example that reanimated the dim religious light of the mother Church. This was especially so with children. When the Establishment largely ignored the pressing needs of the children of the poor, the Evangelicals went to the gutters to seek them and educate them for heaven; when religion was forgotten at home, and treated as a dull piece of unrelated knowledge at school, the Evangelicals insisted that a family not God-centred was Satan-centred, and that religion was the beginning and end of all education; when church-going was a mere routine which children were not expected to take too seriously, and sermons were often a series of pious platitudes, the Evangelicals urged children to church at peril of their souls, and when they got them there they told them to repent or be damned.

In due course, all these ways, except the last, other branches of the Church adopted. No dozer ever admits he has been asleep: the Church of England was no exception. The Sunday-school Movement, begun by the Evangelicals, was soon common property; philanthropy, an especial concern of the Evangelicals, had always been the concern of all, but the Evangelicals wedded it to their heart-religion, and returned the gift with interest. Popular education and religious journalism were both direct results of the Evangelical Revival.

And when all that they began had been disseminated abroad, their own peculiar emphases remained, and if in a limited way—remain still. Children are tainted with the sin of Adam—it is their birthright. Religious education must begin in earliest infancy, to eradicate the mark of the beast; the only purpose of living is dying; the only hope of heaven is to be born again.

REFERENCES

1. Sir James Stephen, *Essays in Ecclesiastical Biography*, II, p. 72.
2. J. Bean, *Family Worship*, p. xxvi.
3. *Poetical Works*, VII, p. 164.
4. Mrs Edwina Gray, *Papers and Diaries of a York Family*, p. 32.
5. *Poetical Works*, VI, p. 403.
6. Ibid.
7. Ibid. p. 404.
8. *Gleanings of Past Years*, VII, p. 225.
9. *Works*, III, p. 315.
10. A. C. H. Seymour, *The Life and Times of Selina, Countess of Huntingdon*, II, p. 88.
11. Ibid. I, p. 115.
12. J. Telford, *Life of Charles Wesley*, p. 269.
13. W. Goode, *A Memoir of the late Rev. William Goode*, p. 4.
14. *Works*, III, p. 239.

15. R. Southey, *Life of Wesley*, II, pp. 221–2.
16. *Memoirs of the late Rev. Basil Woodd*, p. 78.
17. Ibid. p. 99.
18. *Arminian Magazine* (1781), p. 535.
19. Sir James Stephen, *Essays in Ecclesiastical Biography*, II, p. 20.
20. L. Tyerman, *Life of the Rev. George Whitefield*, II, p. 513 and I, pp. 124–5.
21. E. E. Kellett, *Life and Religion in the Early Victorian Age*, pp. 93–4.
22. G. O. Trevelyan, *The Life and Letters of Lord Macaulay*, I, p. 28.
23. L. F. Church, *Early Methodist People*, p. 243.
24. R. Southey, *Life of Wesley*, II, p. 142.
25. *Poetical Works*, VI, p. 419.

Bibliography

THESE are the chief sources. Dates given refer to the edition of the book used; not necessarily the first edition. A large number of tracts are not represented. Where reference has been made to these, the title, author, and date have been put in the appropriate note.

C. J. Abbey and J. H. Overton, *The English Church in the Eighteenth Century* (1878)

W. O. B. Allen and E. McClure, *History of the S.P.C.K.* (1898)

Arminian Magazine

J. Ashton, *Chapbooks of the Eighteenth Century* (1882)

W. Atherton, *Life of Darcy, Lady Maxwell* (1863)

R. O. Ball, *There is Holy Ground ...* (1950)

G. R. Balleine, *History of the Evangelical Party* (1933)

W. T. A. Barber, *Memoirs of the late Rev. William Barber* (1930)

H. C. Barnard, *The Port Royalists on Education* (1918)

—— *A Short History of English Education* (1947)

J. Bean, *Family Worship* (1810)

G. Beebee, *Counsel and Warning to New Converts* (n.d.)

J. Benson, *A Short Account of the Death of Mrs Mary Hutton* (1777)

Joseph Benson (ed.), *Memoirs of the Life of the Rev. Peard Dickinson* (1803)

John Berridge, *Works* (1838)

H. Bett, *The Early Methodist Preachers* (1935)

—— *The Spirit of Methodism* (1937)

R. Bickersteth (ed.), *A Memoir of John Newton* (1865)

T. Bingham, *An Account of the Life and Death of Elizabeth Radder* (1815)

A. H. Body, *John Wesley and Education* (1936)

M. Bowen, *Wrestling Jacob* (1937)

J. W. Bready, *England Before and After Wesley* (1938)

S. Brewster, *The Christian Scholar* (1710)

Y. Brilioth, *The Anglican Revival* (1925)

B. Brough, *An Account of the Life and Death of Mrs Sarah Brough* (1781)

A. Brown, *Notices of the Lives and Death-Beds of Abner and David Brown* (1836)

—— *Recollections of Simeon's Conversation Parties* (1863)

G. Burder, *A Serious Address to Sick Persons* (1786)

—— *The Closet Companion* (1787)

—— *The Good Old Way, or the Religion of our Forefathers* (1787)

G. Burder, *Early Piety, or Memoirs of Children Eminently Pious* (1863)

S. Butler, *The Way of all Flesh* (1903)

W. B. Cadogan, *The Life of the Rev. William Romaine* (1796)

W. R. Cannon, *The Theology of John Wesley* (1946)

W. Carus, *The Life of Simeon* (1847)

E. B. Castle, *Moral Education in Christian Teaching* (1958)

R. Cecil, *The Life of John Newton* (1853)

J. Cennick, *Village Discourses on Important Subjects* (1819)

L. F. Church, *Early Methodist People* (1948)

Children's Monthly Garden

Christian Observer

J. B. B. Clarke (ed.), *An Account of the Religious and Literary Life of the Rev. Adam Clarke* (1833)

W. H. Clarke, *The Psychology of Religion* (1958)

W. K. L. Clarke, *Eighteenth Century Piety* (1944)

J. Cole and J. Parker, *Memoirs of Miss Hannah Ball* (1839)

J. C. Colquhoun, *Wilberforce, his Friends and his Times* (1866)

J. Cottle, *Reminiscences of S.T.C. and R.S.* (1847)

G. G. Cragg, *Grimshaw of Haworth* (1947)

G. Cussons, *His Own Life* (1819)

J. H. Darton, *Children's Books in England* (1932)

J. Dennis, *Southey's Life and Letters* (1894)

S. G. Dimond, *The Psychology of the Methodist Revival* (1926)

T. Dixon, *A brief Account of the Life and Death of Barbara Walker* (1777)

A. E. Dobbs, *Education and Social Movements, 1700–1850* (1919)

P. Doddridge, *A Plain and Serious Address to the Master of a Family* ... (1799)

J. W. Draper, *The Funeral Elegy and English Romanticism* (1929)

G. Eayrs, *Wesley and Kingswood and its Free Churches* (1911)

Maldwyn Edwards, *John Wesley and the Eighteenth Century* (1933)

—— *After Wesley* (1935)

L. E. Elliott-Binns, *The Early Evangelicals* (1953)

Evangelical Magazine

J. Everett, *Wesleyan Methodism in Manchester* (1827)

Family Magazine

H. Fish, *Memoirs of Joseph Pearson* (1849)

—— *Memorials of Mrs Mary Sarson Cooper* ... (1855)

J. Forrester, *Dialogues on the Passions, Habits and Affections peculiar to Children* (1748)

E. M. Forster, *Marianne Thornton* (1956)

Mrs Gaskell, *Charlotte Brontë* (1901)

M. D. George, *London Life in the Eighteenth Century* (1925)

J. Gibbons, *The Mourning Saint among the Willows* ... (1788)

F. C. Gill, *The Romantic Movement and Methodism* (1937)

W. E. Gladstone, *Gleanings of Past Years* (1879)

W. Goode, *A Memoir of the late Rev. William Goode* (1828)

Gospel Magazine

Edmund Gosse, *Father and Son* (1907)

S. B. Gould, *The Vicar of Morwenstow* (1899)

Mrs M. Graham, *Letters on Education* (1790)

Mrs Edwina Gray, *Papers and Diaries of a York Family* (1927)

J. L. and B. Hammond, *The Age of the Chartists* (1930)

—— *The Bleak Age* (1934)

N. Hans, *New Trends in Education in the Eighteenth Century* (1951)

J. A. Hanway, *A Comprehensive View of Sunday Schools* (1786)

—— *A Comprehensive Sentimental Book for Scholars Learning in Sunday Schools* (1786)

R. S. Hardy, *William Grimshaw, Incumbent of Haworth* (1860)

G. E. Harrison, *Son to Susannah* (1937)

Howell Harris, *A brief Account of the Life of Howell Harris* (1791)

James Hervey, *Works* (1789)

Rowland Hill, *Instructions for Children* (1794)

—— *Divine Hymns attempted in easy language for the use of Children* (1794)

—— *Sermons to Children* (1833)

A Short Account of the Death of Elizabeth Hindmarsh (1789)

Henry Home, *Loose Hints upon Education chiefly concerning the Culture of the Heart* (1781)

C. A. Hulbert, *Annals of the Church in Slaithwaite* (1874)

W. Huntington, *Works* (1911)

T. Jackson (ed.), *The Journal and Poetry of the Rev. C. Wesley* (1849)

—— *The Lives of Early Methodist Preachers* (1865)

Thomas Jackson, *Recollections of my own Life and Times* (1873)

William James, *The Varieties of Religious Experience* (1929)

J. Janeway, *A Token for Children* (1753)

William Jay, *Works* (1842)

J. Jefferson, *The Young Evangelist* (c. 1800)

An Account of Mrs Elizabeth Johnson (1799)

M. G. Jones, *The Charity School Movement in the Eighteenth Century* (1938)

—— *Hannah More* (1952)

E. E. Kellett, *Life and Religion in the Early Victorian Age* (1938)

Alexander Knox, *Remains* (1834)

R. A. Knox, *Enthusiasm* (1950)

Vicesimus Knox, *Liberal Education* (1781)

J. Lackington, *Memoirs of the Life of J. Lackington, Bookseller* (1791)

—— *Confessions* (1804)

H. Longden, *Life of Henry Longden, of Sheffield* (1846)

F. W. Maitland, *Life of Leslie Stephen* (1906)

H. F. Mathews, *Methodism and the Education of the People, 1791–1851* (1949)

Methodist Magazine (formerly *Arminian Magazine*)

J. W. Middleton, *An Ecclesiastical Memoir of the first Four decades of the Reign of George III* (1822)

M. Milner, *Life of Isaac Milner* (1842)

G. Monro, *An Essay upon Christian Education* (1823)

Hannah More, *Complete Works* (1830)

—— *Cheap Repository Tracts* (1795–8)

W. Morgan, *The Parish Priest* (1841)

J. Morison, *Founders and Fathers of the London Missionary Society* (1840)

John Newton, *A Monument to the Praise of the Lord's Goodness* ... (1785)

—— *Olney Hymns* (1779)

—— *Memoirs of the Rev. William Grimshaw* (1825)

J. E. Orr, *The Second Evangelical Awakening in Britain* (1949)

G. Osborn (ed.), *The Poetical Works of John and Charles Wesley* (1870)

J. Overton, *The True Churchmen Ascertained* (1802)

I. Parker, *Dissenting Academies* (1914)

J. Pearson, *The Life of William Hey* (1822)

J. B. Pratt, *The Psychology of Religious Belief* (1907)

—— *Remains of the Rev. R. Cecil* (1830)

—— *Eclectic Notes* (1856)

Joseph Priestly, *Miscellaneous Observations relating to Education* (1798)

J. W. Prince, *Wesley on Religious Education* (1926)

F. C. Pritchard, *Methodist Secondary Education* (1949)

W. H. Proby, *Annals of the Low Church Party* (1888)

M. Quinlan, *Victorian Prelude* (1941)

—— *William Cowper: A Critical Life* (1953)

J. E. Rattenbury, *The Evangelical Doctrines of Charles Wesley's Hymns* (1941)

J. S. Reynolds, *The Evangelicals in Oxford* (1953)

L. Richmond, *Sermon ... Cruelty towards the Brute Creation* (1802)

—— *The Dairyman's Daughter and Other Stories* (1908)

J. H. Rigg, *Essays for the Times* (1866)

—— *Reminiscences* (1904)

B. Rogers, *The Cloak of Charity* (1949)

W. Romaine (ed.), *The Works of the Rev. Thomas Jones* (1764)

The Works of the Rev. Wm Romaine (1813)

G. W. E. Russell, *The Household of Faith* (1902)

J. Ryland, *The Preceptor, or Counsellor of Human Life* (1776)

J. C. Ryle, *Christian Leaders of the Last Century* (1899)

W. Sargent, *Battle for the Mind* (1957)

T. Scott, *The Force of Truth* (1779)

M. Seeley, *Later Evangelical Fathers* (1914)

A. C. H. Seymour, *The Life and Times of Selina, Countess of Huntingdon* (1839)

T. B. Shepherd, *Methodism and the Literature of the Eighteenth Century* (1940)

Mrs Sherwood, *The History of the Fairchild Family* (1876)

E. Sidney, *Life of the Rev. Rowland Hill* (1834)

—— *Life of Sir Richard Hill* (1834)

—— *The Life and Remains of the Rev. Samuel Walker* (1835)

J. S. Simon, *The Revival of England in the Eighteenth Century* (1907)

N. G. R. Smith, *The State of Mind of Mrs Sherwood* (1946)

C. Smyth, *Simeon and Church Order* (1940)

R. Southey, *The New System of Education* (1812)

—— *Life of John Wesley* (1820)

W. W. Stamp, *Wesley's Orphan House* (1863)

Sir James Stephen, *Essays in Ecclesiastical Biography* (1907)

Sir Leslie Stephen, *English Thought in the Eighteenth Century* (1881)

G. J. Stevenson, *City Road Chapel, London* (1872)

J. Stillingfleet, *Life of Thomas Adam* (1819)

J. Stonhouse, *Religious Instruction of Children Recommended* (1775)

—— *A Collection of Prayers for the use of Private Persons* (*c.* 1780)

—— *Materials for talking familiarly with Children* ... (1795)

N. Sykes, *Church and State in England in the Eighteenth Century* (1934)

J. T., *Faith Triumphant: Exemplified in the Death of Mrs T——* (1772)

J. Taylor, *Robert Raikes and Northamptonshire Sunday-schools* (1880)

J. Telford, *Life of Charles Wesley* (1900)

An Account of the Death of Mrs Anne Thornton (1799)

Silas Told, *An Account of the Life, and dealings of God with Silas Told* (1786)

Augustus Toplady, *Memoirs* (1813)

Townsend, Workman and Eayrs, *A New History of Methodism* (1909)

Mrs Trimmer, *Fabulous Histories designed for the Instruction of Children* (1786)

—— *Some Account of the Life and Writings of Mrs Trimmer* (1816)

A. S. Turberville (ed.), *Johnson's England* (1933)

L. Tyerman, *The Life and Times of the Rev. John Wesley* (1870)

—— *The Oxford Methodists* (1873)

—— *Life of the Rev. George Whitefield* (1882)

—— *Wesley's Designated Successor* (1882)

A. C. Underwood, *Conversion: Christian and Non-Christian* (1925)

E. T. Vaughan, *The Life of Thomas Robinson* (1815)

H. Venn, *Sermon ... on the death of the Rev. William Grimshaw* (1763)

Henry Venn, *The Complete Duty of Man* (1841)

J. Venn, *The Life and a Selection from the Letters of the late Rev. Henry Venn* (1834)

—— *Forms of Prayer, and Offices of Devotion* (1841)

J. Venn, *Annals of a Clerical Family* (1904)

W. Wait, *The Last Days of a Person who had been one of Thomas Paine's Disciples* (1802)

Samuel Walker, *Fifty-two Sermons* (1763)

J. D. Walsh, *The Yorkshire Evangelicals in the Eighteenth Century* (MS.)

Isaac Watts, *Works* (1812)

T. Webster, *Sermon ... in Consequence of the Death of the Rev. Thomas Robinson* (1813)

L. A. Weigle, *The Training of Children in the Christian Family* (1922)

John Wesley, *Works* (1872)

John Wesley (ed.), *An Extract of Miss Mary Gilbert's Journal* (1768)

Wesley Historical Society Minutes

Westoby (ed.), *An Exposition of the Four Gospels* (*T. Adam*) (1837)

T. White, *A Little Book for Little Children* (1702)

J. H. Whiteley, *Wesley's England* (1938)

R. Whittingham, *A Memoir of Rev. John Berridge* (1838)

R. I. Wilberforce (ed.), *Family Prayers by the late William Wilberforce* (1831)

R. I. and S. Wilberforce, *The Life of William Wilberforce* (1838)

W. Wilberforce, *A Practical View of the Prevailing Religious Systems of Professed Christians* (1797)

S. C. Wilks, *Memoir of the Rev. Basil Woodd* (1831)

Basil Willey, *The Eighteenth Century Background* (1946)

D. Wilson, *A Sermon occasioned by the Death of the Rev. Basil Woodd* (1831)

W. Winter, *The Life and Writings of Augustus Toplady* (1872)

T. Wood, *The Season of Youth favoured with the Divine Presence* (1814)

Memoirs of the late Rev. Basil Woodd (1834)

Memoirs of Mrs Hannah Woodd (1784)

J. Wright, *Spiritual Songs for Children* (1796)

Index